All Together Now

All Together Now

Connected Communities:
How They Will Revolutionize
the Way You Live, Work, and Play

Paul Hoffert

Stoddart

Published in 2000 by Stoddart Publishing Co. Limited
34 Lesmill Road, Toronto, Canada M3B 2T6

Distributed by:
General Distribution Services Ltd.
325 Humber College Blvd., Toronto, Ontario M9W 7C3
Tel. (416) 213-1919   Fax (416) 213-1917
Email cservice@genpub.com

04   03   02   01   00   1   2   3   4   5

Canadian Cataloguing in Publication Data
Hoffert, Paul
All together now
Includes index.
ISBN 0-7737-3228-4
1. Community life — Technological innovations. 2. Electronic villages
(Computer networks). 3. Computer networks — Social aspects.
4. Technological innovations — Social aspects. 5. Community.
6. Social participation. I. Title.
HM756.H63 2000   307   C00-930031-7

Jacket Design: Angel Guerra
Text Design: Joseph Gisini/Andrew Smith Graphics, Inc.

THE CANADA COUNCIL | LE CONSEIL DES ARTS
FOR THE ARTS | DU CANADA
SINCE 1957 | DEPUIS 1957

*We acknowledge for their financial support of our publishing program
the Canada Council for the Arts, the Ontario Arts Council,
and the Government of Canada through the
Book Publishing Industry Development Program (BPIDP).*

Printed and bound in Canada

This book is dedicated to my immediate connected community: Brenda, David, Brian, Mei, Karyn, Quinton, Serena, and Jorel. They remind me of the primacy of family and social relationships. The fact that we are all together now has contributed greatly to the book's creation.

Contents

Preface

THE MOST POPULAR NON-ACTION COMPUTER GAME OF THE 1990s was SimCity, which allows players to design the infrastructure of a city and see whether it becomes a desirable place to live. The software simulates sewer systems, water supplies, schools, taxes, and so on. SimCity and its successors are engaging because they give us power over social, economic, and political systems over which we cannot normally have great influence. Controlling parameters that directly affect the lives of people is as close as most of us get to playing God.

In 1994 I had the opportunity to design a real community, one that would be distinguished by its digital connectivity. My colleagues and I studied the evolution of towns, cities, and neighbourhoods throughout the world and tried to synthesize that historical information into a trial of future living that would have an impact on many aspects of work, play, and family life. After assembling the significant resources needed to design and build the neighbourhood, its digital network, and content that would interest the residents, we directed a research effort that monitored the impacts of the connectivity. The residents were ordinary suburban families, neither "early adopters" nor "propeller-heads."

As the research results began to accumulate, it was clear that many things were going on in this community that were not anticipated. The biggest surprise was that, when we superimposed our digital network onto this neighbourhood, the residents used their electronic connectivity in very different ways than people use the so-called "virtual" communities on the Internet. Our neighbours discussed lost pets, babysitters, a teachers' strike, the local real estate developer, and a host of other mundane issues. Internet discussions rarely deal with local issues, because participants don't live in the same neighbourhood.

On the other hand, our residents knew each other. They signed their real names to their communications and viewed each other in their video-phone conversations. There could be no "spoofing," or pretending to be someone else, and this imbued their conversations with more relevance and trust than is seen on the Internet.

Because our network was private, residents made friends and shared personal facts more freely. They arranged to meet for a beer at the local pub. Many teenagers began to teach technically challenged community members how to use their computers and software, and became a local, free technical-support resource.

We made videos that demonstrated the wide range of advanced applications and content that our residents used, featuring residents speaking about their experiences. They spoke candidly about the everyday problems in modern life and how some of these had been overcome in their community. I maintain a busy schedule of speaking engagements around the world, and I began inserting some of these videos into my presentations. I found that, no matter which group I was addressing and no matter which topic I was presenting, when it came time for the audience to ask questions, the great majority focused on the interactive community trial.

This held true for technology presentations to semiconductor companies, e-commerce presentations to retailers, intellectual-property presentations to lawyers and governments, and information technology presentations to librarians. Everyone wanted to know what people actually did when they lived in a community that was outfitted with the appliances, connectivity, and content we will all have in the future.

I began to search for other community trials throughout the world that connected residents with digital networks. I was fascinated to find that our key findings were replicated in very different circumstances and in very different cultures. As I continued to accumulate this data, I gravitated to the idea of writing a book about how communities will develop in the twenty-first century. *All Together Now* is the result.

In addition to exploring the experiences of those who have tasted the fruits of the digital revolution, I have documented the historical context of recent changes and predicted some of the potential — perhaps inevitable — impacts.

Many of my academic colleagues, along with large numbers of the media and the population at large, are concerned that the digital revolution will somehow de-humanize us — turn us into zombies glued to our computer screens, uninterested in face-to-face contacts. This image is fuelled by pundits, who predict a new century characterized by cocooning individuals staying at home and shunning social interactions.

But this is not what we or others have found to be the case. In fact, people who live in connected communities find them to be the friendliest places they have ever lived. And they have more face-to-face encounters than those of us who live in unconnected neighbourhoods. The digital technology and increased communications are bringing these people closer together, not driving them apart.

That's not surprising. The ability to interactively communicate facts, thoughts, and emotions is a distinguishing feature of humanity. Along with tool-making, it separates us from the other inhabitants of our planet. I believe that the latest communications tools are creating a revolution that will make our neighbourhoods more social and more rooted in family values than those of the industrial era we are leaving behind.

I've coined the word "habicons" to describe these new connected communities. As you will see, they will change the way you live, work, and play in the coming decades.

Paul Hoffert
Toronto
March 2000

PART ONE

The Need
for Habicons

CHAPTER 1

Drop Out or Tune In

THEODORE WAS A BRILLIANT MATHEMATICIAN. HE HAD TAUGHT at the University of California, Berkeley campus, and was very adept at computers and other technologies. But he had rejected these in favour of a solitary life away from the hustle and bustle of the modern world, in a simple cabin near Lincoln, Montana, where he could bask in nature and control the elements of his existence. His living and working space was a single room devoid of modern appliances save for an old manual typewriter on which he had written a manuscript expounding his philosophy.

> *Section 1. The Industrial Revolution and its consequences have been a disaster for the human race. They have greatly increased the life-expectancy of those of us who live in "advanced" countries, but they have destabilized society, have made life unfulfilling, have subjected human beings to indignities, have led to widespread psychological suffering (in the Third World to physical suffering as well) and have inflicted severe damage on the natural world. The continued development of technology will worsen the situation. . . .*
>
> *We attribute the social and psychological problems of modern society to the fact that society requires people to live under conditions radically different from those under which the human race evolved and to behave in ways that conflict with the patterns of*

behavior that the human race developed while living under the earlier conditions.

Among the abnormal conditions present in modern industrial society are excessive density of population, isolation of man from nature, excessive rapidity of social change and the break-down of natural small-scale communities such as the extended family, the village or the tribe.

For primitive societies the natural world (which usually changes only slowly) provided a stable framework and therefore a sense of security. In the modern world it is human society that dominates nature rather than the other way around, and modern society changes very rapidly owing to technological change. Thus there is no stable framework. . . .

In modern society an individual's loyalty must be first to the system and only secondarily to a small-scale community, because if the internal loyalties of small-scale communities were stronger than loyalty to the system, such communities would pursue their own advantage at the expense of the system.

The system! That was the problem. The damned system had evolved as if it were a sentient being, driven by its own ego and need to survive. The people who created the system had become secondary to the infrastructure. Before the age of industry had engulfed the world, small communities nurtured their residents with a sense of place, a sense of belonging, a feeling of security. Nature was close at hand. It was something to be respected, to be cultivated and harvested, but not to be vanquished.

Theodore's cabin held his bare necessities: a thin mattress bed in the corner, a lone table, a small shelf for books, a few pots and pans. No toilet. No electricity. No light bulbs. No heat. But while Theodore lacked the amenities of modern life, he had traded them gladly for a far greater prize — his personal freedom. He had power over the important aspects of his life: his food, his shelter, and his security. He relied on no supermarket, no landlord, and no police force. No one could turn off the electricity, no one could turn off the cable TV, no one could refuse to fix his car, and no boss could tell him what to do.

But Theodore was not just a technologically challenged Luddite who dismissed computers and the Internet for their complexity. He was, in fact, a master of technology who had foregone its bounties for his philosophical belief that personal freedom is more important than the benefits bestowed by modern conveniences.

> *Section 117. In any technologically advanced society the individual's fate MUST depend on decisions that he personally cannot influence to any great extent. A technological society cannot be broken down into small, autonomous communities, because production depends on the cooperation of very large numbers of people and machines. Such a society MUST be highly organized and decisions HAVE TO be made that affect very large numbers of people. When a decision affects, say, a million people, then each of the affected individuals has, on the average, only a one-millionth share in making the decision. . . .*
>
> *Thus, permanent changes in favor of freedom could be brought about only by persons prepared to accept radical, dangerous and unpredictable alteration of the entire system. In other words, by revolutionaries, not reformers.*

A shelf in Theodore's cabin held a row of containers, each one carefully labelled in his own hand. One read "Experiment 97," another "Potassium Chlorate." Others were filled with timers, electronics, fuses, and other bomb-making materials. These bits of technology, oddly incongruent with the pre-industrial flavour of the place, were tolerated for a very special purpose.

Theodore (Ted) Kaczynski was the infamous Unabomber, named for his early targeting of *un*iversities and *a*irlines, the most wanted criminal in the United States. Between 1978 and 1995, he sent bombs disguised as parcels, boxes, pipes, and road hazards to professors, a geneticist, an advertising executive, computer stores, and several universities across the United States. Over a nearly twenty-year period, he had outsmarted and befuddled law-enforcement officers at every level of government. Three people had died from his efforts, and an additional twenty-six had been maimed, crippled, or wounded. The toll would have been much higher if not for some misfires and other lucky breaks for his intended victims.

His own luck ran out on April 3, 1996, when FBI agents converged on his cabin in Montana and arrested him. He is currently serving a long jail sentence. If he ever gets out, I hope he doesn't mind that I extracted some of his work.

Kaczynski is a dangerous and maniacal criminal, but some of the ideas he espouses resonate with sane, law-abiding citizens today. He is not alone in feeling alienated from the society in which he lives, but his responses have been hurtful, not helpful, to others and have ensured that his words would have no impact on improving the conditions he deplored. The extracts from his manifesto were chosen not just for their relevance to this book, but also to illustrate that his choice of action resulted in no good end, not for him or for anyone else.

His observation that the Industrial Revolution had negative effects on families and communities is generally accepted by historians of technology. Workers had to follow the work, so when large factories appeared as centres of employment, these became magnets for townsfolk and rural residents seeking to better their economic situations. Men had to uproot themselves from their local communities and relocate around industrial complexes. If they left their wives and children in their home communities, their family ties became weakened. If they moved their families with them, they left behind the families' traditional community support structures.

The technologies of industrialization created engines that could drive ships and trucks, which in turn required networks of rivers, lakes, seas, and land routes. These paved the way for companies to increasingly operate in national and international settings, with offices and factories situated in several cities. Frequent relocation of personnel followed this growth of national and international commerce, now uprooting middle- and upper-level sales and management people, who had to pull their children out of school and leave their friends and families behind for new cities in which they had no ties.

It is at this point of the argument that Kaczynski and others make an erroneous leap of logic, for they associate the artifacts of the Industrial Revolution with those of technology in general. This is tantamount to associating the artifacts of farming, the pre-industrial revolution, with those of industrialization, and it makes no sense. The technology of agriculture, for example, *created* communities, and it certainly helped stabilize the family unit. Although Kaczynski and his ilk do not generalize the negative aspects of industrialization to farming, they do not hesitate to associate these with the new technologies of digital connectivity.

The current digital revolution, however, is fundamentally different from industrialization because it brings products and services to people, not vice versa. In that regard, it has the reverse effects of industrialization, and allows for decentralization, deregulating, and diminished advantages to living in a downtown urban environment. The impacts on local communities and family life will, as a consequence, be quite different from those of industrialization.

Parents today may lament the fact that their children can access information on the Web that they deem inappropriate, but at least they are doing so at home, subject to their families' influence, rather than downtown or at a mall. More people are able to work at home today, and more parents are able to stay at home to look after their children than at any other time in the past century. Fewer people work in factories or large, faceless companies. A growing number are self-employed and control where they live. In short, the Industrial Revolution is over, and the world's wealth is increasingly being created by the manipulation of various forms of information and entertainment.

The new technologies, which are based on digital connectivity, are changing the way we live and work. Their impacts, like those of the Industrial Revolution, will be enormous, but they will be different from the social upheavals that occurred in the past two hundred years.

The call for a simpler way of life, with an increased connection between what we do and its end result, resonates within us all. Disintermediation — the elimination of middlemen — is, at the beginning of the twenty-first century, beginning to accomplish that end, bringing suppliers closer to customers and citizens closer to governments. As decentralization, downsizing, deregulation, and interactivity take hold, the distance between makers and users begins to diminish.

The future shock emanating from the proliferation of information, a direct result of the technologies of printing and mass communications, has already arrived, and the only solution to the problem of information overload involves taking a new and revolutionary path back towards generalization and away from specialization. The seeds of this change are already underfoot, nurtured by Internet-like networks that allow us to get just-in-time information without having to acquire it in advance of our need. Meanwhile, our computers are beginning to cull the masses of data so that we will receive *less* information and entertainment than we do today.

Less is certainly better at this point. We don't want more e-mail and we don't want more television channels. There is not enough time to peruse the information and entertainment that exist, let alone plunge into the expanded choices that are becoming available. We want less, but we want it targeted at us individually: *what* we want and *when* we want it. The integration of new media, computers, and communications promises to do just that: decrease the amount of unnecessary trivia we have to deal with and leave us more time to concentrate on things that are important to us.

Kaczynski's assertion that "a technological society HAS TO weaken family ties and local communities if it is to function efficiently" is simply not true. The technology of the water well allows people to live farther apart from each other, getting water on their own property rather than going to the communal river, while the technology of the supermarket brings a large number of people together, creating its own community of place and purpose. Each has its own advantages, disadvantages, and effects on community life. The appropriate question to ask, therefore, is whether a particular technology is community-friendly or not. As we will see, the connection of neighbourhoods by high-speed networks can reverse the industrial impacts on community living.

I find it curious and relevant that right-wing radicals like the Unabomber espouse the same courses of action to rid the world of technology as do the leftist radicals whom they detest. David Noble, a York University professor and a leftist historian of technology, suggested on a CBC Television program that he would do *anything* to stop the deployment of the Internet, even using force, if necessary.

Obsessions with the evils of all technology are dangerous, not only for the damage that radicals can occasionally inflict, but also for the basic misunderstanding they convey about human nature and tools. The use of technology is an essential part of being human. Tools are natural outcomes of our intelligence, and they separate us from other animals. They are not inherently bad, but they are capable of inflicting horrific damage if not used wisely. Knives can be used to harvest crops, but they can also be used to kill people. Digital watches can be used to tell time, but they can also be used as countdown devices to detonate bombs.

The way in which a new technology is used is crucial to the impact it will have. Those who suggest that we should boycott and attack the process invite an outcome that is the opposite of what they hope for. By attacking those who wish to harness the new tools to restore powerful family and community ties, they ensure that their views will be excluded as the new infrastructures are set up.

This book examines communities connected with modern digital networks, real-life examples of the technology that some believe will further depersonalize and dehumanize us while destroying the vestiges of nuclear families and family values. The evidence and arguments presented in these pages, which are based on early trials in communities connected in this manner and other evidence gathered from Internet use, are mostly to the contrary. They indicate that it is more likely, in fact, that twenty-first-century living will bring a return to the importance and pivotal roles of local communities and families. As far as individual freedom is concerned, the Internet has empowered individuals in a manner not thought possible ten years ago. The turn of the millennium can reasonably be described as a time when free enterprise is rampant and individuals can increasingly conduct their lives outside the control of large industrial-era corporations, unions, and governments. If you doubt this, consider that Internet transactions escape local sales taxes.

The simultaneous trends towards both globalization and localization are a key to understanding the new reality. In a sense, these opposing trends represent the conundrum of the digital age: how do we increase the power of the highest level of infrastructure (multinationals), newly empower the lowest (ordinary citizens), and neuter the middle managers who have characterized so much of the civilized world's twentieth-century progress?

CHAPTER 2

Localization within Globalization

THE WORD "COMMUNITY" IS COMMONLY TAKEN TO MEAN either a place where a group of people live or the group that lives there. Communities first gained importance after humans began farming, because that activity rooted them to a single location around which collective enterprises could more easily thrive.

Connected communities, our living and working places for the twenty-first century, are enabled by new information routes, which are consequences of the digital revolution. They are beginning to replace the urban, suburban, and rural communities that were enabled by automobile, railway, and airline routes, consequences of the Industrial Revolution.

The most exciting aspect of connecting physical neighbourhoods with digital network infrastructure is that such a network overlays a real community of people living in close proximity with virtual communities like those on the Internet. The results are different from those that can be achieved by either of these communities in isolation, and are sometimes even counterintuitive.

We'll Provide the Hot Dogs — You Bring the Drinks

Here's an example of what can happen. In 1996, I directed a connected community trial in a suburban neighbourhood of Newmarket, Ontario. Residents said it was the friendliest place they had ever lived. When participants first moved in, we asked if they would share their e-mail addresses with their neighbours. After they agreed, we created a type of community bulletin board, a listserv, which sent e-mail to everyone in the neighbourhood when any one of them posted a message.

While it's true that there are thousands of listservs on the Internet, the members they serve do not generally cohabit a physical neighbourhood, so they have no opportunity to meet and share a beer. Research on the use of video conferencing has shown that the mediated experience of communicating on a network is much more meaningful after users have established a trusting, face-to-face relationship. In our trial, we were able to accomplish this by mapping the *physical* community onto the *virtual* community using an intranet — a private community network — with significantly different results from those of Internet use.

Think for a moment about your own neighbourhood. If you've read this far, you probably use e-mail. Chances are good that many of your neighbours have e-mail. Chances are also good that you don't know most of your neighbours, and that you never communicate with them. The simple reason? You don't know their e-mail addresses. Even if you wanted to make your own e-mail address available, you would have no easy way to keep that information private and prevent marketers (and worse) from getting hold of it.

In the Newmarket trial neighbourhood, one of the earliest messages posted was this: "Barbecue at our house Friday night. Everyone invited. We'll provide the hot dogs. You bring the drinks." The result was a terrific get-to-know-your-neighbours party where almost everyone met face to face.

Could this have happened without the neighbourhood intranet? Not easily. The resident who initiated the party was a member of the local police force and worked shifts. He would have had to go door to door, ringing or knocking and hoping that his neighbours would be at home at the times he was off work. Some folks would have been out shopping or at a movie. Others might have been working or visiting friends. Some kids might have been home with instructions not to answer the door if a stranger came by. The bottom line is that this type of social event rarely takes place any more. It's too much trouble to organize and implement. But in our cyber example, the party-thrower wrote the e-note invitation in about one minute, the neighbours read it when it was convenient for them, and almost all the community residents showed up for the bash.

This anecdote contradicts trend-spotter Faith Popcorn's cocooning metaphor, which suggests that residents will increasingly remain indoors, glued to their televisions and computer screens at the expense of face-to-face social interaction. The experience in New-market and other connected community trials has been that people within these neighbourhoods are more social and meet face to face more frequently, not less.

Connectivity in the Global Village

Although we speak of the new revolution as a digital one, perhaps its most meaningful effect is connectivity. At the heart of digitization is interoperability, the ability for systems and people to work together. Digital systems can interoperate because, at their heart, they speak the same language of ones and zeros. And when systems can be connected, people will connect them. The resulting connectivity is taking place on a level that makes Marshall McLuhan's "global village" catchphrase seem like a gross understatement.

This new connectivity has the potential to be much more democratic than the older model. It will be easier for ordinary people to connect to information routes than it was for folks whose communities were left off the auto and air routes of the twentieth century. Some may dispute this last statement, arguing that the cost of connection to the Internet has been a barrier to use, thus creating a world of info-rich and info-poor. But I believe it is reasonable to compare digital connectivity with the deployments of telephone and television networks in the twentieth century. These have penetrated all strata of our society, and are accessible by all. They provide a good model for democratic Internet access. You may not like certain television programs or telephone solicitations, but they reach the rich and poor alike, regardless of sex, race, or ethnicity.

The connectivity of mass media has been asymmetric, with just a handful of radio, television, newspaper, magazine, and book companies controlling the information that is force-fed to the billions on our planet. The old mass media framework was predominantly a framework of few to many: mass communication, mass marketing, mass production, and so on. The new connectivity, on the other hand, is essentially symmetric and configurable: one to one, one to many, few to many, and so on. It is also interactive, so we can supply information as well as receive it. We can be *on* television, not just watch it.

The symmetric — some would say democratic — nature of interactive networks is both a blessing and a curse. We all love our newfound power and control over the digital media. On the Internet, we can get sports scores whenever we like, without waiting for the evening television news or the morning newspaper. But although they like the freedom it supports, most users are appalled at the lack of Internet regulation. Web sites that contain child pornography, explicit sex scenes, hate-mongering, and instructions on how to build bombs (even nuclear ones) are high on users' lists of those they want off their screens, or at least off their kids' screens.

The issue is central to the new connected communities because they are by definition local, not global. What makes a neighbourhood cohesive is its local culture, not a subscription to the vague concept of a global society. In order to create and foster local culture, it is necessary to maintain unique values and contexts that separate the local community from the teeming hordes of *everyone else* out there in the ether. Unless we encourage a return to localization, we will be left with the legacy of late-twentieth-century communities: being connected with the whole world and yet feeling alone, lacking the close relationships and support provided by pre-industrial communities. In order to move on, we must find ways to hive off our local networks from the global Internet and provide private and comfortable havens for our families and friends.

Empowerment of Individuals

The Industrial Revolution was characterized by mass production, mass marketing, centralized power, big brother governments, and powerful unions. It is giving way to the digital revolution, with its personalized products, targeted marketing, decentralized governments, and empowerment of individuals.

The movement of power and control from the centre of systems to their edges is detailed in my earlier book, *The Bagel Effect: A Compass to Navigate Our Wired World*. Briefly, the forces of deregulation, downsizing, decentralization, digital convergence, and interactivity had, at the close of the twentieth century, produced major disintermediations in companies, governments, religions, schools, and social systems. As middlemen and their proxies have been eliminated, individuals have gained increasing control over their work and play. The power vacuum at the system centre leaves a hole that makes the traditional organization circle look like a bagel. The important action has moved from that now vacant centre to the edges of the organization, the periphery where interactions with customers, clients, citizens, members, and end-users takes place.

The signs are everywhere. Communism, the centralized stepchild of the Industrial Revolution, has floundered. Businesses have become more customer-focused. Governments are smaller, have fewer resources, and are moving programs and responsibilities back to citizens. Mainframe computers have given way to desktop computers. The centrally controlled broadcast networks are being usurped by narrowcast, viewer-driven channels devoted to golf and home improvements. Telephone networks, intelligent but also very expensive, are giving way to computer-type networks that can be much simpler — that is, dumber — because the computer appliances at their edges are smarter than telephones. The new network designs are one thousand times cheaper than the old ones, and they are wresting control from the centralized telephone companies — the telcos — and putting it into the hands of users.

The positive results of these changes have been partially masked by the inevitable short-term upheavals and insecurities that come with massive change, but the signs are clear that we are entering a new era of increased opportunity and prosperity. Perhaps the greatest beacon of the future has been the Internet, which has all power and control vested in its "netizens" at the edges of the system, with little administrative power or control at the centre.

A Phone Network Grows in Brooklyn

I grew up in Bensonhurst, a residential neighbourhood in Brooklyn, New York, but my family moved out in the mid-fifties. I returned twenty years later with my wife to show her my old stomping grounds, and I was impressed with how little my old street had changed. Not only did the houses look the same as I remembered, but everything was in perfect condition, from the carefully manicured lawns to the immaculate cars, somehow unscathed by the normal New York rack and ruin.

A few years after my trip back to Brooklyn, a neighbour from my youth paid a visit to my home in Toronto. He recounted the recent history of my former abode and solved the riddles posed by my return visit. As it turned out, the mob began buying houses on my old street shortly after my family moved out. One by one, they purchased all the homes until the entire street was an enclave of organized crime. My friend's parents sold their house some dozen years after we moved out, when they received an *offer they couldn't refuse*. By the time I made my pilgrimage, the street had become a private community with invisible gates at each end. There was no petty crime, and residents could leave their front doors unlocked without fear of theft. Cars were not scratched or scraped. Those who, in ignorance, transgressed the mob's unwritten local etiquette met with violence.

My friend made a most interesting observation about the community's connectivity. It seems that the residents, concerned about wiretaps and other intrusions on their privacy, had connected a private telephone system, with all the wiring on their properties (which were staked with No Trespassing signs). Their private telephones were separate from the public telephone system and did not interoperate with it. Their segregated phones couldn't be used to call out of the street, but no one outside the street could tap into them, either.

Of course, mobsters are not the only ones who are concerned with privacy. I have attended many conferences filled with law-abiding citizens for whom privacy is at the very top of the agenda. And today we have a similar capability to privatize conversations and information within our local digital networks using intranets, which are hived off from the public Internet by computer firewalls that can be programmed to let traffic in and out selectively. As connectivity becomes pervasive, these private networks will increasingly become part of the digital fabric, taking their place alongside today's public Internet.

But will these private networks ghettoize netizens in much the same way that gated communities of the late twentieth century did to their residents? Today's physically gated communities prevent unwanted criminals and outsiders from coming in, but they also transform these communities into ghettos. You cannot visit a friend at a gated building or neighbourhood without a pass or word being left with the security guard. In this way, our most expensive residences have come to resemble prisons more than they do carefree living.

Electronic gates, on the other hand, allow a community to let in and out as much traffic as it may desire. A community intranet, for example, can give residents full access to the global Internet while keeping out unwanted lurkers and loathsome web sites. The key question we must ask now is what the outcome of Internet technology will be, and how that may be tested against our hoped-for objectives. Here we can take a cue from what may seem an unlikely source.

The Amish

Amish and Mennonite communities have become hot topics for discussion among the "digerati" because they raise important issues that relate to how our electronically connected communities may develop.

Howard Rheingold, an author and long-time proponent of on-line communities, returned to the Pennsylvania counties of his youth to document Amish perspectives on communities and new technologies. The Amish present old-fashioned conservative images, with their horse-drawn carriages and drab outfits, and have become a cliché for communities that reject modern technology. They sew their own clothing, cultivate their fields with horse-drawn ploughs, and manage to live happily in houses that lack electricity.

But Rheingold found that Amish attitudes towards technology are not as simple as they seem. Instead of rejecting the use of technologies outright, the Amish believe that each tool should be evaluated on the basis of how its use affects the community. This important relationship between technology and community goes to the centre of Amish culture. They are not against the use of all modern tools. Gas barbecues and other contemporary appliances are used, but only if these first pass muster in an elaborate system of evaluation.

These communities typically divide themselves into groups of about twenty-five families, with each group making up a "district" represented by a bishop. The bishops meet twice a year to discuss, among other things, which technologies may be used in their districts. Their conclusions may not agree with yours or mine, but their reasoning illuminates issues that are worth everyone's consideration.

To test the appropriateness of a technology, for example, the bishops ask, "Does it bring us together or draw us apart?" Donald Kraybill, author of *The Riddle of Amish Culture*, notes, "You find state-of-the-art barbecues on some Amish porches. Here is a tool they see as bringing people together." Many Amish even used automobiles for a time. But after much discussion, it was decided that cars were encouraging Amish to travel too far beyond their extended families, and were thus diverting their attentions to non-community recreations. The bishops felt that this activity decreased social cohesion and personal connection, both of which are central to the Amish way of life, so the use of automobiles was restricted.

A central issue for the Amish is connectivity to the outside world, which they generally refer to as "the English." If a technology, like electricity or the telephone, requires that the community rely on external organizations, such as public utilities or governments, it is generally forbidden. The thought of allowing a company or a government to have a control over your life by metering and possibly turning off your electricity or telephone is anathema to these self-sufficient folk.

So most Amish communities do not permit the use of electricity. But when electricity is the only means of running power tools in a workshop, for example, some bishops authorize the use of so-called Amish electricity. Here's how they make it: diesel fuel is hauled in a horse-drawn cart from town and then used to run a farm generator that charges a bank of batteries. These, in turn, are connected to a converter that creates the local 110-volt AC current required by the tools. Because it is expensive and difficult to operate, this complicated system discourages the general use of electricity. It restricts the use of radios and televisions, which would otherwise be hot links to the "English" world.

It is appropriate that we "English" also ask ourselves whether new technologies will draw us closer together or tear our communities apart. In the twentieth century, we too frequently restricted ourselves to asking the single question, "Does it make money?"

Connected Communities Then and Now

It's not surprising that we find it difficult to predict the impact of connected communities. A century ago, we were introduced to new technologies that had dramatic impacts on connecting communities, and back then no one was able to predict the outcomes, either.

When the automobile was introduced, for example, it was hailed as a substitute for the horse and buggy and was given the appellation horseless carriage. No one envisaged that automobiles and the network of highways they spawned would lead to the development of entirely new types of neighbourhoods — suburbs and exurbs. Our cities and commuter towns of today are the direct result of automotive travel, but car manufacturers had no idea their products would spur these radical changes in lifestyles.

Alexander Graham Bell, inventor of the telephone, did not foresee that his new appliance would become an indispensable mode of communication. His commercial vision was rather that the telephone would be a consumer entertainment, with one telephone set at Carnegie Hall, say, and thousands of others in residential homes throughout the New York area. Customers might pay a percentage of the live concert ticket price to listen to a Puccini opera in the comfort of their own homes.

When we consider these examples, it seems not surprising that so many pundits have been getting it all wrong. Many have been adamant that connectivity will be characterized by entertainment traffic. Others have maintained that consumer and business transactions will drive connectivity in the coming years. Still others believe that only advertising can generate a high enough revenue stream to pay for the required infrastructure.

It is much more reasonable to assume that the new networks will follow the history of telephone networks, which have no single killer application. The killer application is *everything*. You talk with friends, family, neighbours, business associates, and customers; you book holiday travel, make an appointment with a doctor, or chat on a sex line; you send and receive faxes, log on to the Internet, and transfer financial data; you send e-mail or file an electronic story from a baseball game.

Telephones are pervasive simply because it is too scary for most of us to contemplate life without them. Although we want the cost of communications to go down, we would pay double or triple the current rates if faced with disconnection. Don't think so? That's what we paid just a few years back, and no one disconnected.

Tomorrow's communities will be characterized by ubiquitous digital connectivity that people will not be able to do without. Some connections will be wired, others wireless. Today we can easily envisage new technologies encompassing the services provided by television and telephones, but their ultimate value will be much higher. One of the new perspectives is that we are connecting people, not just appliances. Whatever the future will bring, it will be experienced with more simultaneity and by a larger fraction of the earth's human population than ever before.

CHAPTER 3

Communities Lost

SOME ARGUE THAT THE DIGITAL REVOLUTION HAS OBVIATED the need for local communities. Instead of separating ourselves into smallish groups, we should, according to this thinking, embrace the global communities of commerce, pan-nationality, and cyberspace, while applying the U.S. ideal of a cultural "melting pot" and homogenizing the billions of souls on our planet into an extended family of humankind. Unfortunately, embracing that ideal without a concomitant re-establishment of local communities would destroy our sense of cultural heritage and belonging.

The perpetrators of this genocide of local culture attempt to substitute the structures of nation and business for those of family and community. The result of replacing the close-knit smaller structures with larger structures that lack personal relationships has been that people feel less rooted in their communities and less responsible to their neighbours, and this has been reflected in increased crime and family neglect.

The problem of re-establishing strong local communities has been evident throughout the industrialized world, but it is not generally recognized as a problem with an easy solution. In the existing vacuum, commercial enterprises have sprung up to provide some of the security, friendship, trust, and shared experiences that we crave. The so-called club floors offered by hotel chains are one such commercial amenity. For a higher room charge, travellers can stay in a partitioned-off area of the hotel that has its own sitting room with free fruit, drinks, juices, snacks, breakfast, and an honour system for noting if you consume extra-cost items such as hard liquor.

When I couldn't afford the luxury of such accommodations, I believed them to be a rip-off, a commercial exploitation of people's desire to one-up their colleagues and massage their egos, a snooty way to exclude the riff-raff from the vicinity of those who can afford better.

When I became a frequent traveller, however, flitting from city to city for a day or two stay in each, and as my clients began to be able to afford the cost, I started using these accommodations, which gave me a new perspective on these mini-communities and shed light on the value of localization. The experience of staying in a club room is more akin to that of staying in a bed and breakfast — that is, quite different from the faceless, undifferentiated accommodations of normal hotel life.

The local concierge at the gate of the club floor remembers my name when I check in and speaks with me familiarly for the duration of my stay (even if it is only one night). Other travellers who frequent the sitting room occasionally exchange pleasantries or chat with me as they look up from their newspaper or coffee, and the friendly feeling is somewhat like sitting at home with my family. These fleeting bits of civility from people whose faces and voices become recognizable make my visits more pleasant and memorable.

The temporary club communities are built not only on the common experiences of travellers, but also on the physical proximity that is shared. We chat about local weather, news headlines, or the quality of the hors d'oeuvres. The normal "bubble" of no touch, no talk, and no eye contact that surrounds us in unfamiliar environments is generally absent.

That cocoon of protection, born out of our fear of those who are outside our community, has been one of the most negative effects of industrialization, which uprooted individuals from their familial communities and relocated them where the factories were. The problem was exacerbated when national and international companies began moving administrative and sales people from city to city without regard for the uprooting of children from their schools and families from their friends and relatives. As women entered the workforce and governments increasingly assumed responsibility for our sick and elderly, our relationships became fewer, looser, and less focused on providing the trust, security, and intimate communications that bring us emotional stability.

I've had other experiences with temporary local communities. In 1969, I founded a rock band, Lighthouse, with Skip Prokop and Ralph Cole. They had been in travelling bands before, but it was my first time away from home. For the next four years I was on the road almost constantly, playing hundreds of different venues in a single year.

I had travelled before, but I'd never been away from my wife and children for more than two days at a time. All of a sudden, I was going away for six weeks at a stretch, coming home to a family that had grown accustomed to life without me, re-establishing a bond for a week or two, and then leaving again.

I had been a loner — shy by nature, awkward in social situations, and fearful of being with more than two people at a time. In short, I was like many other performers, acting on stage as a way to connect with others while protected by the proscenium arch and a persona that I wore like a mask.

The problem was that I was incredibly lonely away from my family and friends. While some of my bandmates partied late into the night at local bars and clubs, I languished in my hotel room. I spent my free time in the light of day going to museums, planetariums, and other local sights. I was gaining a fantastic knowledge of the history, geography, and culture of American and Canadian cities, but I wasn't having much fun. It was great to play at Carnegie Hall in New York, Expo 70 in Japan, and the Isle of Wight Festival in England, but I wasn't getting to know the local people. After almost a year of playing on the same shows as Jefferson Airplane, Elton John, Bob Dylan, Miles Davis, the Who, Joni Mitchell, and Jimi Hendrix, I hadn't spoken a word to any of them. I decided things had to change.

In order to have even a fleeting relationship with someone you will know for only a day or two, you have to be outgoing and friendly, able to start up a discussion and then continue it. Faced with self-imposed hermitage as an alternative, I taught myself how to do it.

While I never became the life of the party, I found that I could strike up a conversation with a hotel clerk or cab driver and find someone at a party with whom I shared at least a passing interest.

As soon as I learned to communicate with strangers, I started to relate better to the members of my own band. Lighthouse had thirteen musicians: four horn players, four string players, four in the rhythm section, and a lead singer. We also travelled with a road manager, a sound mixer, and a crew of three who set up, tore down the equipment, and drove the truck.

These eighteen people became my family on the road, and the dynamics were remarkably like those of my family and friends at home. At any given time, I would be particularly close to a few, while the others were kept at distance in case of a disagreement that would trigger temporary changes in the makeup of my inner circle.

I felt, with my bandmates, a much stronger level of trust, a heightened feeling of belonging, and a greater sense of security than I did in the rest of the world at large. I would defend them to others, even in the wake of a falling-out among us. I realized that the term "band" was not accidentally applied to both aboriginal tribes and groups of musicians.

My experience is not unique. People in the theatre, in circuses, and in the armed forces build strong local communities based on their shared experiences and geography, although the geographical location is a constantly moving venue.

Once I started talking with box-office people, fans, other performers, and anyone else I met, it was easy to get a sense of the social upheaval that was endemic in the 1960s. The hippie movement was largely an expression of young people's frustration with the lack of fellowship and community in mainstream life. By dropping out, whether for a weekend or for a few years, participants found alternative communities that gave them the care, trust, and support that were lacking in their traditional community settings.

The same phenomenon has been evident in the 1990s in the rave movement, in which thousands of young people converge on a location, which is usually kept secret until the last moment, to dance, prance, and trance away the night in a loving, drug-induced haze reminiscent of hippie bashes of thirty years earlier. In the 1999 documentary feature film *Better Living Through Circuitry*, John Reiss captures the importance of these temporary communities to the participants and shows how they contrast with the lack of community in their ordinary home and work experiences.

Rave participants speak of the common bond of trust and fellowship they share, regardless of social or economic background, and about the love and spirituality they find, particularly when their experiences are enhanced by drugs such as ecstasy (the so-called love drug). The failure of twentieth-century families and local communities to provide these important emotional anchors has driven many away from the mainstream and into activities that are seen as extreme and dangerous.

At the same time, the most positive development in twentieth-century communities — the advent of cyber-communities — took place as the millennium wound down and the Internet wound up. These cyber-communities are bringing a new sense of connection and relevance to many members of the same demographic groups that have been alienated by modern desocializing trends.

CHAPTER 4

Communities On-Line

INSTEAD OF CONVERSING WITH MACHINES AND DATABASES, PEOPLE are increasingly using computer networks to connect with other people. These networks have become social halls, and they are occupied by virtual communities that require no physical space, do not encroach on each other, and never go to war because they outgrow their resources.

Communities in cyberspace, although they cannot replace local face-to-face relationships, have begun to offer netizens significant benefits. They offer forums for narrow interest groups whose views might not garner sufficient numbers to be expressed within smaller local communities.

There are three general types of on-line community: virtual communities of interest, communities within organizations, and local communities on-line. Let's look at each of these in a little more detail.

Virtual Communities of Interest

Virtual communities of interest are examples of what academics call computer-supported social networks. These are people — tens, hundreds, or thousands — who will likely never meet face to face but share a common interest or concern. It may be a hobby, a political viewpoint, or a religion. It may be a rare illness, an aspect of computing, or the Internet. The possibilities are endless.

The participants in virtual communities of interest have no

common culture or background, and it is not unusual for an individual's interest in participating to wax and wane. The main tools used by virtual communities are mailing lists, Web conferences, and newsgroups.

Communities within Organizations

Organizations increasingly use intranets — private internal networks that use Internet protocols — to enable staff to collaborate more effectively. The activity that takes place is known in the lingo as computer-supported collaborative work.

Workers may be sitting at adjacent desks or communicating across the globe between different offices within the same organization. Their communications tend to be focused on organizational business and specific tasks, and are generally conducted within the organizational culture.

My experience at CulTech, the research centre I directed for eight years, is that these intranets are also frequently used for more humorous and frivolous pursuits — passing on Internet jokes of the day and such. In some organizations, network administrators often eavesdrop on worker activities and admonish those who are "wasting time."

Local Communities On-Line

Many neighbourhoods, villages, towns, and cities now have their own web sites that mirror some of the real activities that take place locally. Although these are in some sense virtual communities of interest, they are distinguished by the fact that participants are also likely to meet each other face to face, and thus use the connectivity to enhance their proximal relationships. These local on-line communities are the focus of several subsequent chapters.

When my grandson was having serious behaviour problems in kindergarten, my daughter-in-law went on the Web to seek information about his problem. Was he just a bad kid or were other children experiencing similar problems? She quickly found that her five-year-old fit perfectly the set of characteristics of children whose physical, emotional, and intellectual development are out of sync with each other. These children all exhibited the same problems at school, problems that stemmed from the lack of intellectual challenge within their peer group and their inability to cope with the structured environment at school.

He was no longer alone. She was no longer alone. Thousands of kids had gone through that problem stage, and within a few years their minds and bodies had come back into sync and the problems had vanished. That left nothing to worry about except how to help him through a few tough years.

Within a few days, more comfort and assistance appeared in the form of a cyber-community made up of parents whose children shared the same problems and experiences. My daughter-in-law made pen-pal friends with some of the parents, and she found a community of shared interest and experiences that was unavailable to her locally.

Although today's cyber-communities offer a large and diverse array of unique group experiences using a variety of technologies, these are still in the early stages of development, using text almost exclusively as the method of conversing with others. We are in the equivalent of the Elizabethan era of cyber-communications, a period in which letter writing forms the bulk of our correspondence.

Within the next few decades, however, the Internet will also embrace voice and video traffic. Imagine the impact of merging the technologies of radio, telephony, and television and layering their capabilities onto the Internet, which is already the most important communications and community-building technology ever introduced. But before we jump to the future, let's examine what's available today.

E-mail

There are two types of network-enabled communications. The first is asynchronous, or time-shifted, and the most common example of this is e-mail. Someone may have sent you an e-mail message hours or weeks earlier, but you can reply to it whenever you are available without losing the thread of the communication.

E-mail provides the ability to send a message, note, letter, graphic document, audio, or video to another person or a group of people. It is quickly replacing regular (snail) mail because it can provide the same functions more quickly and at a reduced cost. Like snail mail, e-mail allows the sender to compose messages as carefully as may be required before sending. But e-mail is essentially less formal than paper mail.

The number of e-mail messages sent daily already exceeds the sum of telephone calls and faxes sent daily. This should not be taken as evidence that low-bandwidth text services are deemed adequate for communication on digital networks, but as proof that the advantages of Internet communications are so great that users prefer this mode of communication even though they can access only a tiny fraction of its potential.

The heart of mail technology is the formal structure needed to fit messages into the confines of pieces of paper. Whether you are writing freehand on a piece of personal stationery or printing your word-processed document on a standard 8.5-by-11-inch sheet, the font size, paragraph style, and line spacing are constrained by the physicality of the page and the way your text and graphics are arranged on it.

Your thought processes are also channelled into the types of communication elements that can be best expressed by text on paper — sentences, paragraphs, salutations, and the like. The medium does influence the message, as Marshall McLuhan noted, and in letter writing a key aspect of the medium is that the recipient gets to see the message exactly as formatted by the sender. The sender controls all of the formal elements. In the case of Web-based e-mail, formal control moves from the sender to the receiver.

The receiver's e-mail program settings, not those of the sender, control the formatting, including the font type, the size of characters, line spacing, line width, number of characters in a line, number of lines on a page (in a window), and so on. This means that, in general, there is not much point fussing over the formatting of a message the way you might for a letter, since the recipient of your e-letter will not see the fruits of your labour.

Although the functions of mail and e-mail are similar, then, the inherent structure of e-mail has caused it to evolve towards a much less formal grammar and style. What we see is a more immediate form of text expression, one approaching that of everyday speech. Contrast this with our expectation that every letter we receive in the mail should be free of spelling, syntactic, or formatting errors (no second pages with a single line on them, please), lest it reflect badly on the sender. Composing an e-mail message is therefore much quicker than composing a physical letter. This ease of use has helped spawn a return to written messages, a mediated form of communication that dominated human interactions for hundreds of years.

Telephone service was responsible for the great decrease in letter writing in the twentieth century, and this has been linked, along with television viewing, to a decrease in print literacy. On the other hand, the newer technology of e-mail has arguably created a dramatically more literate community of users.

Because we create and send e-mail so quickly (no paper to fold, envelopes to seal and address, or letters to take to a mailbox), we use it far more frequently than regular mail. This has reversed the trend away from letter writing, returning us to the days when personal communications were primarily conducted through text. Furthermore, with e-mail, the mediation is less strong than with the older print technologies, so the written words become almost coincidental with speech.

Some are concerned that the new literacy does not use the same grammar, syntax, and vocabulary as the older physical forms, but this fails to acknowledge that literacy is medium-dependent, varying even within the print media of newspapers, magazines, textbooks, novels, and so on. As an academic, I am competent at writing and reading articles published in academic journals, but this certainly does not mean I have the literacy required to read (or write) a Harlequin Romance.

Like most other artifacts of connectivity, the new form of correspondence will not completely replace the older form, but it will significantly cannibalize its use. Connected communities will certainly use e-mail more than mail, but people will still want to use printed letters for contracts, formal invitations, and other documents where precision and control by the sender are important.

It is safe to assume that everyone who has a telephone today either has or will soon have an e-mail address. It is also safe to predict that most of those who do not currently have telephone numbers will soon have e-mail addresses. As telephony and computer networks converge, the Internet system that delivers your e-mail today will soon incorporate telephone services, making it a no-brainer for underdeveloped countries to decide which infrastructure should be deployed. Telephone networks are becoming an anachronism that will disappear in a few short decades.

Listservs, Newsgroups

You can send a letter to only a single address because physical things exist in a single location. With e-mail, on the other hand, it's easy to send your message to as many recipients as you wish, simply by adding names to the address field. Most people who use e-mail for business find it useful to group addresses together under a single label, so they can send a message to everyone working on a particular project, for example, with a single name entry.

The natural evolution of group addresses in e-mail was the list-serv. (The truncated spelling of this name dates back to the days when eight characters was the maximum number one could use in a file name. In the incredibly accelerated timeframe of digital-network development, it seems inconceivable that only a few short years ago it was necessary to truncate the spelling of words and names — and thought processes — to accommodate computer memory limitations.) A listserv is a companion application to e-mail. The application reads various fields in an e-mail message (From, Subject, Message, etc.) and, working in conjunction with the e-mail server, performs simple tasks according to instructions programmed by the owner.

The most frequently performed tasks are to add a new member's name to the list (SUBSCRIBE), to delete the name of a member who no longer wishes to be on the list (UNSUBSCRIBE), and to make your message available to list subscribers (POST). With these three basic commands, almost anyone can start and maintain a powerful, automated, and interactive publishing activity.

In many connected communities, a listserv is the major source of up-to-date information about local news and events. A private person or a public employee may be tasked with maintaining a community listserv. Residents wishing to be informed about community matters subscribe simply by sending an e-mail message to the listserv address with the word SUBSCRIBE in the subject line.

In an unmoderated system, any member can send a message that shows up as e-mail for all subscribers. The Guild of Canadian Film and Television Composers, of which I am president, supports vigorous conversations among our members with almost no administrative cost. We use several listservs for member communications. One list is for the executive and a second is for all members. Because our list is unmoderated, any message sent to the appropriate address from a subscribed member (in our case, someone who has paid his or her dues) shows up in everyone's mail. We have to remind new members that messages such as racy jokes are unwanted by some members and are therefore not appropriate for posting.

In moderated lists, all messages from members show up at the moderator's e-mail. Only the moderator has permission to post messages to the subscribers to the list. While this is somewhat totalitarian, well-moderated lists are among the most popular because users receive little spam (unwanted mail).

Another form of list management is the newsgroup. These are similar to the listserv in function, number in the tens of thousands, are generally unmoderated, and pump out messages posted by any member. Members who abuse their privileges are generally added to a *persona non grata* list that "unsubscribes" them in perpetuity.

E-mail, newsgroups, and lists are called push technologies because when you open your computer application, any messages addressed to you are automatically shown on your monitor. The AOL message, enshrined in the movie title *You've Got Mail*, is a good example of the intrusive nature of these communications.

BBSs and Text Conferencing

Bulletin board systems (BBSs) are also known as conferencing systems. They are technologies for informing users about topics of interest. While listservs are constantly pushing messages to your e-mail, BBSs require that users take the deliberate action of accessing the bulletin board and logging in with a user name. In this case, there is no subscription to a membership list. It takes a pull from the user to access the information.

Bulletin boards predate the Internet. Initially, they required that you phone a special access telephone number, which then connected you through a modem to a computer at the BBS site. These have all but been replaced now by web sites, since the Web can offer similar services and is accessible by standard browsers without the need for a special program and a dial-in telephone number.

Most BBSs allow participants to create topical groups in which a series of messages (called threads) can be strung together one after another. There are several popular conferencing systems, including Usenet, the Well, Echo, and the discussion groups of America Online and the Microsoft Network. Each sustains a wide collection of topics of discussion and lively ongoing give-and-take between participants. Tens of thousands of people already contribute hundreds of thousands of messages to these conferencing systems *every day*, in countries throughout the world and in languages that range from Innu to Chinese.

After I wrote *The Bagel Effect*, my publisher set up a bulletin-board forum that allowed visitors to comment on topics raised in the book. I was given the power to moderate comments and place them within conference threads to help focus the discussions. When a visitor sent a comment, I would receive an e-mail alarm informing me of the forum that had activity. I would log onto the book's web site forum, read the comment, decide if it should be publicly posted and whether I wished to post my own reply within the public forum.

The closest physical world comparison to these cyber-communications may be special-interest and trade magazines such as *Fine Woodworking Hobbyist* or *Orthodontists Monthly*. The comparison is weak, however, because these commercial ventures are funded by advertising and subscription sales, are generally unavailable to casual readers, and have no mechanism (other than short letters to the editor) for subscribers to publish their material for other subscribers. In contrast, Internet-based communications are free, easily available to any user familiar with a search engine, and provide an interactive platform for interested persons to make their views and information known to others.

When you immerse yourself in the culture of cyber-connections, it becomes clear that for a large majority of users, the issue of personal control and empowerment is as important as the feature-set of the communications tool. The mass media have so castrated individual contributions to large and small debates that there is pent-up demand for systems that allow people to contribute, sometimes to vent, about any topic they can (and do) imagine.

Let's Chat

Each of the previously discussed forums — e-mail, lists, newsgroups, and BBSs — are asynchronous, which means that contributors do not have to be on-line at the same time. Users interact by making comments in turn, but a reply may occur minutes or months after the previous posting. There are some benefits to asynchronous interaction, the prime one being that members can interact without everyone gathering at a particular time. This time shifting becomes essential when people are on different schedules or live in different time zones.

But synchronous (real-time) conversations among people are the hottest action on-line, the activity that frequently drives first-timers to buy a computer and shell out a monthly fee to an Internet service provider (ISP). Surprise, talking is popular! In the vernacular, this is called chat. Whether your chat is text-only (most of it is today), audio (like speaking on the telephone), or video, it requires that you react to messages as they are conveyed from others involved in the communication or entertainment.

If you compare e-mail with the postal system and listservs with bulletin boards, then chat would be compared with CB radio. Like CBers, people who use chat scan channels of conversations until they catch something of interest, then they lock in to that channel and join in. Most chat systems support a great number of "channels" dedicated to a vast array of subjects and interests.

Chat does not generally take place on the Internet, because Internet protocol (IP) is not fine-tuned for real-time activities. Nonetheless, for most users chat is associated with the Net, since it travels over the same digital networks and requires no additional connection. Text chat requires a centralized computer application — that is, a server that grants its owner power over access to the system and to individual channels.

In commercial services such as AOL or the Microsoft Network, chat channels are generally policed by the provider's staff or by appointed volunteers, who make certain that conversations do not exceed the arbitrary limits of good taste (known as netiquette) set by the provider or legal limits set by the courts.

The largest non-commercial system — Internet Relay Chat (IRC) — offers free software for PCs (MIRC), Macintosh computers (IRCLE), and other computer platforms, allowing conversations to take place among all who log in, without regard for their technological creed. Each channel has an arbitrator, known as an owner, who has the authority to admit or eject people from the conversation, and who can decide how many may participate at any time. Being chosen as an owner for an IRC channel is an honour usually bestowed on an individual who has participated frequently and has been judged worthy by his or her peers.

Chats have used the lowest common denominator of network communications technology — text — so they may be available to the widest range of participants. Like the other communication forms I've described, text greatly limits the ability of users to express themselves. Unlike asynchronous activities, however, chatters do not have the relative luxury of composing their messages before they are sent, and this has encouraged the development of a wide range of shorthand expressions that are used to indicate complex emotions with just a few characters. These generally represent facial expressions, and are constructed from standard keyboard characters such as parentheses and colons. Following are a few of these shorthand expressions that strike me as inventive or humorous. (You must mentally rotate these images ninety degrees clockwise.)

:-) or :)	Smiling face
:-}	Smiling face with lipstick
;-) or ;)	Smile and a wink (means you are playing or flirting)
~~:-(	Angry (flames coming out of head)
#-)	Partied all night
:-(*)	Feel like vomiting
:^(	Nose put out of joint (useful for replying to flames)
:-p	Sticking one's tongue out
l-)	Asleep or bored
:-o	Shocked
:-#	Lips are sealed
:-@	Screaming

Flinging MUD

The acronym MUD stands for multiple user domain/dungeon. MUDs are similar to chats, except that they fit the metaphor of architectural space instead of a CB radio (in other words, channels are generally replaced by rooms). The model of a physical space allows for many additional contextual elements that can make a session more involving. MUDs originated from adventure-style games in which a player is represented by a fictional character who has to navigate through rooms filled with dangerous enemies, objects, and various forms of treasure. The player moves through the rooms, picks up and drops objects, and overcomes obstacles such as a vicious dragon or a baffling puzzle.

MUDs, one of the oldest forms of computer games, gained new functionality in the 1970s, when digital networks first enabled players to play with and against other players. Since then, some of these have evolved into very sophisticated and complex games. Although MUDs began as a type of entertainment, they are evolving into simulation tools that may be used by communities to solve thorny municipal problems (which can be presented as obstacles that must be overcome within the simulation). At the same time, many "social" MUDs have become a means for widely dispersed groups to maintain personal contact.

MUDs sometimes incorporate other networked communication, such as e-mail and discussion groups, to provide links among the players. They are similar to text chat in that they allow for interactions among netizens in real time. Communication is usually restricted to users who are currently in the same room.

Like e-mail lists, MUDs are typically owned by the individual or group that provides the hardware, the software, and the technical skill needed to maintain the system. These owners are known as gods because they decide which participants are given administrative controls (those selected are called wizards) and how many computer and network resources are allocated to each user. Because a god determines a user's access to rooms, communications, and virtual attributes, participants in MUDs develop sophisticated social systems and hierarchical relationships.

Although chats, bulletin boards, conferences, forums, MUDs, lists, and e-mail all predated the World Wide Web, the technologies they use may be mimicked within an ordinary web browser. The disadvantage of incorporating these communications into the Web is that it was not designed for real-time personal communications, but rather for accessing and linking documents presented as web pages. As a result, a browser is usually not as efficient at handling these communications as the other stand-alone programs mentioned.

On the other hand, the Web is excellent for integrating graphics, sound, and moving images with text, and in this area the other programs are generally very weak. So as Internet users move to higher bandwidths with the adoption of cable-modems, telephone DSL (digital subscriber line), and high-speed wireless access, the Web will increasingly take over much of the virtual community traffic. If e-mail is any indication, these functions will be glued onto browsers (as Netscape's Messenger does, for example). They thus appear to users as a single integrated application, even though the underlying technologies may be quite different.

Role-Playing, Honesty, and Avatars

In direct conversations, the identity of each speaker provides the context for deciphering the messages and meanings couched within the spoken words and phrases. When the president of a nuclear-weapons facility says to the commander-in-chief of the armed forces, "Push the button now," for example, it has a very different meaning from the same command a child gives a parent in a pinball arcade.

Context and identity are not ancillary to meaningful conversation but are essential elements. And this raises an important question about the nature of conversations mediated by the Internet because they are currently text-based (and thus offer no identity or context for those having the conversation). Is your child talking to another child on the Web, or is he talking to a pedophile?

Direct conversations bring a wealth of cues and clues about the identity of those with whom you are speaking. Clothes, voice modulation, physical appearance, gestures, and the environment in which you meet all convey messages about status, power, trustworthiness, and group membership of the speaker. This explains why video conferencing has not been particularly effective when the participants have never met each other, though it does supply some of the visual information of a direct conversation. On the other hand, when participants have met face to face prior to the video conference, they have already established a much stronger sense of identity and trust, and the communications are much more meaningful.

On the Internet, however, all bets are off, and that brings advantages as well as problems. One of the most endearing aspects of the Net is the democratization of text-only communications, which means that someone in a wheelchair, a young girl, a member of a racial minority, and a seasoned business executive can all express themselves in a group conversation without differentiating biases. But when we are having a direct conversation with a group of people we know, we automatically turn to certain individuals for comments and visual acknowledgements because we know who has wisdom, who is objective, and whom we can count on to support us.

In direct conversations, the force of a strong personality frequently determines how much "air time" a speaker gets. The words of someone with a steady gaze and self-assured demeanour generally merit higher consideration than those of someone whose eyes are constantly darting and who seems ill at ease. Net mediation has removed those considerations and given everyone the same chance to air their views without prejudicial bias.

However, there is one aspect of netizens' physicality that has proven important to carry over to Web conversations: gender. Gender seems to be as crucial an indicator on the Web as it is in direct conversations, perhaps even more so. "Are you male or female?" is such a common question that it has been abbreviated to "RUMorF?" in netspeak. It is interesting that there appear to be no similar abbreviations in use for indicating one's age, height, weight, bankroll, or the like.

Judith Donath, in *Communities in Cyberspace*, examines how truthful and counterfeit identities are established in on-line communities. She notes that some identities are easier to fake on-line than in direct circumstances. An example is conspicuous consumption as a means of displaying wealth. A poor or middle-income person has difficulty arriving in a chauffeur-driven limousine, living in a mansion, and wearing very expensive clothes, but someone in an on-line chat room can pretend to have those material things without being exposed as a fraud.

One of the few clues for authenticity on the Net is your e-mail signature, which is a combination business card, advertisement, and indication of your personality (signatures frequently include quotes, which may be pithy or funny). By providing your phone number, fax number, address, and/or web site address, you offer some verifiable information that may be used to authenticate your on-line persona.

The issue of listing a web site address in your signature file is interesting because it requires a good deal of effort to establish and maintain a Net presence. As in real life, only a few will go to the trouble of creating and maintaining all the trappings of a false identity.

The poverty of contextual information is a limitation for trustworthy transfers of messages, but it also enables interactions that are enhanced by one's ability to pretend to be someone else. This has encouraged role-playing, not only in the highly popular MUDs and games, but also as part of network interpersonal communications.

A Cyber Love Story

My nephew Jon participates in many of the networked communications that have been discussed in this chapter. A few years ago, he was frequenting a chat group using a bogus persona he created because he wanted to protect himself from unwanted recognition and, presumably, because he thought it was fun to assume a false identity. He pretended to be an older married man with a family. In that guise, he met a (supposedly) married woman in a chat channel and had a number of interesting conversations with her.

After a few days of communal chat, they began to split off from the larger channel and converse privately, gradually peeling off the protective layers of their alter egos and revealing their true personalities and situations. After two weeks of private chat, they felt confident enough to exchange telephone numbers and establish voice contact. This was a big move, since your telephone number can be reverse engineered to find your real name and address.

They found out that neither was married, that he was a heterosexual man and she a heterosexual woman, and that they were about the same age. Lorie lived in Texas and Jon lived in Toronto. For the next ten months, they got to know each other very well through a combination of continued chat, occasional phone calls, and even snail-mail letter writing, which allowed them to exchange photographs.

Almost a year after Jon and Lorie first contacted each other in a chat channel, my sister mentioned that Jon was going on vacation to Texas. "Why Texas?" I asked naively. "It seems he has a friend there," she said. "Met her on the Internet." "Cool," I said, wondering if Jon would be picked up at the airport by a chainsaw-wielding ex-con in drag.

They hit it off. Like old-fashioned pen pals of yesteryear, they had spent a great deal of time exploring how they felt about important issues and had conversed about very personal matters, perhaps more personal than they might have dared raise in a direct dating circumstance. By the time they met face to face, they felt like long-time close friends. In fact, they had known each other for a year.

Two months after Jon's trip, Lorie gave up her job in Texas and moved to Toronto, into Jon's apartment. They were married almost another year after that, with Lorie's family contingent arriving from southern Alabama, complete with their own guitar picker. The wedding was fabulous, and it brought together members of Toronto's Jewish community with our new relatives from the far-flung South. Lorie was quickly integrated into our family, although it took her a while to realize that barbecue spareribs are a Chinese dish in Toronto, not the slow-cooked, sauce-drenched delicacy of the deep South.

Was their cyber-courtship less open and honest than it might have been had they met in a bar? Was it more? Would either of them have found a lifetime partner in such a faraway place and foreign culture if it hadn't been for the chat? Does anyone else care? If so, why?

These questions are asked by cyber-sociologists (yes, they do exist). The surrogate personas that people adopt on-line are not very different from those we create when we go to a singles bar or an event where we wish to make an impression. In a direct experience, we alter our clothes, demeanour, and associates, and sometimes create a fictitious context for ourselves (we're the secretary who elevates her status to executive assistant). On-line there is a kind of honesty to the deception, since role-playing is an accepted part of the chat experience.

The advent of the Web's graphic capabilities has led to new and advanced forms of role-playing, primarily through the use of avatars. Avatars are cyber-surrogates, or alter egos, that represent users to others on the network. A user chooses from among a number of faces, hats, clothing, and other attributes that help create a look and a personality for the avatar. The avatar appears on remote screens, complete with a physical appearance and other sensory clues (such as sound effects or a human voice).

The Palace is an advanced MUD that adds avatars to the more usual arsenal of text personas. As you move from room to room, you encounter images of others, and as your avatar approaches another avatar in a room, it elicits a conversation as naturally as you would when approaching another guest at a party. Visitors to the Palace — and these may be scattered around the globe — see and can socialize with each others' avatars, perhaps moving outside to the pool for a swim one day and inside for a game of pool the next.

These technologies may be easily extended for other, more

mundane purposes. Your local city hall could be modelled on-line, for example, and you could roam the halls and wander into the legislative chambers, permit offices, and the like, encounter cyber-attendants, learn about municipal affairs, and conduct business in a much more congenial way than going through an answering-machine rigmarole.

Counterpoint: What's Missing?

Not everyone believes that cyber-communities are beneficial. Stephen Doheny Farina is one of their many critics. In his book *The Wired Neighbourhood*, he points out that "networked virtual realities individuate us, . . . encourage us to ignore, forgo or become blind to our sense of geographic place and community." He goes on: "In immersing ourselves in the electronic net, we are ignoring our real, dying communities. . . . We do not need electronic neighbourhoods; we need geophysical neighbourhoods, in all their integrity. . . . Shared interests are not enough."

Cyber-communities, as Farina envisions them, are similar to the club-floor communities of travellers I detailed earlier. He believes that public spaces in a virtual world "closely resemble an airport bar: it may have bartenders, it may serve drinks, it may even have a brass rail and a piano, but most connections among its clientele are fleeting and its purpose is primarily to offer momentary gratification to transient individuals."

One can argue that this is a valid and useful, if not perfect, community. After all, how many physical communities provide all of our social and emotional needs? Farina raises a further point however, that is difficult to refute. "In physical communities we are forced to live with people who may differ from us in many ways. But virtual communities offer us the opportunity to construct utopian collectivities — communities of interest, education, tastes, beliefs, and skills." The loudmouth who tries to disrupt an on-line community will quickly be ejected by the moderator and prevented from returning, but a similar personality in your physical community must be tolerated unless he or she breaks a serious law. Farina argues that learning to live with people of different values and experiences fosters more tolerance than retreating into a world in which only our own values are mirrored back to us.

Perhaps the most pronounced weakness of on-line communities will never be overcome. Communications will always be mediated, never direct, and thus will always lack the integrity of face-to-face communications. It's one thing to converse with someone about building model airplanes and quite another to meet your hobbyist friends on a Sunday afternoon and go flying. There is no substitute for meeting a buddy for a beer or having friends over for a dinner party.

David Ehrenfeld, in his book *Pseudocommunities*, notes that "when we virtualize human relations, we are no longer in touch with the essential ingredients of community, for at the end of the day when you in Vermont and your email correspondent in western Texas go to sleep, your climates will still be different, your soils will still be different, your landscapes will still be different, your local environmental problems will still be different, and — most importantly — your neighbours will still be different, and while you have been creating the global community with each other, you will have been neglecting them."

But this bleak vision is not the only scenario, nor is it the most probable one.

CHAPTER 5

Community Neighbourhoods

WHY SHOULD WE BOTHER TRYING TO RE-ESTABLISH THE physicality of neighbourhoods when the connected world presents an opportunity to do away with them? Well, let's explore why physical neighbourhoods are still important.

Following are three items of interest to fishers. The first, published in 1999 by the *Alabama Fisheries News*, was of great interest to local shrimp fishers but few others.

> *It seems that El Niño has finally subsided, but his evil young sister La Niña appears poised to take his place causing wanton destruction and altering of field schedules! She may become the brunt of blame for the world's evils for some time to come as her brother was for the past few years!*

The second item, published in *Fisherman's News*, September 1999, was of vital interest to local Alaskan crabbing communities:

> *A group of around 150 members of the Bering Sea/Aleutian Islands (BSAI) crab industry met with members of the Alaska Department of Fish and Game (ADF&G) and the National Marine Fisheries Service (NMFS) to listen to an explanation of why many of them may no longer be in the crab harvesting business in the very near future.*

The third, filed by the Canadian Press (CP) in October 1999, was about the Nova Scotia and New Brunswick lobster fishery:

Fisheries Minister Herb Dhaliwal said . . . 33 of 35 native bands have agreed to honour a 30-day voluntary moratorium on lobster fishing while Ottawa comes up with interim guidelines to regulate the fishery.

The events noted in these three fishing communities, each one on a separate coast of the North American continent, could radically affect every aspect of local life, including whether the towns will survive or die. Still, the impact of these stories is not crucial for global villagers outside the communities. Even within the North American fisheries, one set of local events may not have much impact on those in another location.

At each location, these stories generated considerable interest and discussion. They illustrate the need for local community infrastructure in a global world. Although we want access to information about events that are remote from us, we relate much more strongly to the people and context around us.

A Work Community

I've had first-hand experiences that have influenced my views on local communities. Since 1986, I have maintained an office on the Keele Street campus of York University in Toronto. York University was founded in the 1950s at a suburban location, which was meant to take the load off the downtown University of Toronto. By the 1980s, it was still in the middle of nowhere with respect to Toronto cultural activities, although the student body had grown to more than 40,000, the population of a decent-sized town.

Good restaurants, good shopping, art galleries, movie theatres, and the like were not within walking distance, and hardly any were within driving distance. There was lots of green space between buildings, but there was no "main street" where students and faculty could sustain a physical community. In the evening, the campus emptied and felt more like an archeological restoration than a living community. It was clear that a large localized population did not, on its own, constitute much of a community.

By the early 1990s, however, the university's president, Harry Arthurs, spurred the construction of a campus mall that connected several of the central buildings. It provided the "main street" place of congregation that had eluded the campus previously. Now there was hustle and bustle, benches where students and faculty could sit and chat, protection from the elements in winter, and an array of shops and activities that drew the local community together.

Stalls selling trinkets, cheap clothing, music CDs, watches, and posters gave the area a bazaar-like atmosphere, with hawkers collaring passers-by to sell them their wares and political agendas. Now there were diverse restaurants serving Japanese, Korean, Middle Eastern, and Chinese foods plus a fast-food strip with the more mundane burgers, pizzas, fried chicken, and tacos, as well as coffee, muffin, and doughnut shops.

There were clothing stores, a hair salon, a pharmacy, a doctor, a dentist, an optometrist, banks, a travel agency, a post office, a computer store, a copy/instant print, odds and ends, and the campus bookstore. There was also a pool hall, complete with video and pinball games, that stayed open until midnight. The pool-hall trade encouraged a few restaurants to stay open late as well, prolonging activity into the night and providing a sense of security for those of us who worked late or lived in student residences.

Gradually, my experience at the York University campus changed. I opened an account at the local credit union and began to get my hair cut and my teeth cleaned at the mall instead of downtown. I began to work late on campus, doing some reading while dining at the local eateries, watching a few innings of baseball while having a burger at the pub, and shooting a game of pool when my body tightened up from too many hours in front of my computer screen.

I got to know the guy who ran the computer store. He would order software, put it aside for me, and leave me a message when it came in, and I would pick it up when I passed the store. The woman proprietor of the Japanese restaurant, appreciative that I was a regular customer, routinely put an extra free item on my tray. When my first book came out, I gave her a copy as a Christmas gift. I began getting my medical prescriptions filled at the drugstore, got to know the pharmacist, and asked if she could find a cheaper supplier for my arthritis pills. A few days later she told me that her chain did not carry alternatives, but that she had asked a friend at a health-food outlet to pick up a cheaper variety and send them over. She provided these to me at her cost, as a courtesy.

Staff in the stores that I frequent know me by name, and I've become acquainted with faculty members who lunch and dine at the same spots that I haunt. Many faces have become familiar. I have come to know who many faculty members are, even without exchanging words with them, because one or another of my colleagues knows them, points them out, and offers me tidbits of professional information or gossip. In short, my workplace community of interest has become a local neighbourhood for me, and its members have become an extended family.

My Home Community

Shortly after my wife, Brenda, and I had our second child, we decided to buy a house. We didn't have much money at the time, so our choices were somewhat limited. We found a house that suited our needs and price point, but it was in a neighbourhood that neither of us liked. I had lived nearby, and had unpleasant memories of growing up in that recently built suburban environment, far from the downtown action most teenagers crave. The neighbourhood ranked one on a scale of ten when it came to charm, interest, identity, or resources a young person would want to access.

After weighing our options, however, we decided to buy the house as a "starter" because we could afford it. Our plan was to move on to a better neighbourhood as soon as our finances would permit. As it turned out, we never got around to moving. Our kids made friends at school and always nixed any suggestions that we move out of the neighbourhood. By the time they were out of high school, we had constructed an addition to the house, made many other improvements, and landscaped a beautiful yard and patio, making the house more comfortable to live in.

Finally, about thirty years later (time flies when you're having fun), we decided to move to a larger house, one that could accommodate Brenda's ageing mother, as well as our son, our daughter-in-law, and their two children. By this time, we could afford to move to any neighbourhood we wished. But when we began balancing the pros and cons of our neighbourhood, it turned out that things had changed a lot since we moved in.

Lawrence Heights (as it came to be called) was originally near the upper edge of the city. Since we first moved there, however, Toronto had doubled in population and now we are in the thick of things, about the same distance north of the downtown core as we are south of my York University office. We are only two blocks from a subway station and many bus routes. More than a dozen different varieties of fresh bagels are available at bakeries within a five-block radius. Mexican, Italian, Greek, Hungarian, Israeli, Thai, Japanese, Korean, seafood, steak, and three provincial Chinese restaurants are within five minutes of our house. A new library has been built within walking distance, and there are video-rental stores and more than a dozen theatres within a medium walk or quick drive.

Brenda's experiences in the neighbourhood essentially replicate mine at York. She knows the bank tellers, the bakers (yes, they give her a free cookie and such), and the florist, who has become a good friend and philosophical sparring partner. My daughter-in-law, a sculptor, teaches art as a volunteer at her daughter's public school because they no longer have a budget for a paid art teacher. She and my son know many of the moms and dads in the neighbourhood because they meet them at the local playgrounds or hockey rink.

Although Brenda and I originally wanted to move out of the area when it had not yet developed the desirable attributes of community, our children loved growing up there because that was where their friends were. Many of them, including our other son and his wife, came back after their schooling to establish families in the old neighbourhood. Today, many of their friends from primary school have also moved back, and their children are growing up as second-generation friends in the same community.

A few years ago, we bought a new house just six blocks from our old one. I didn't even have to change my telephone number. My postal code is almost the same.

While my experiences cannot necessarily be extended to others, I find that most of my friends and associates place great stock in the quality of the neighbourhoods in which they live. Sometimes the neighbourhood consists of an apartment building or condominium complex, and sometimes it's a small town within commuting distance of work. In each instance, the residents are acutely aware of how connected or unconnected they feel.

Considering the number of Nobel Prizes given to economists for inventing valuation systems for esoteric elements of our economies, it is mind-boggling that no one has ever won a prize for figuring how to value the sense of security, well-being, comfort, and (dare I say?) happiness afforded by a good local neighbourhood.

The associations I have with the place I live and the place I work are very important to me. Although my on-line communities travel with me on my frequent trips, it always feels great to come home. But what happens to local community life when neighbourhoods are connected to digital networks? In the following chapters we will examine some exciting projects that are under way.

PART TWO

Early
Sandboxes

CHAPTER 6

Freenets and Habicons

A S WE'VE SEEN, THE CREATION OF NEW TWENTY-FIRST-CENTURY communities is driven by global connectivity, which creates virtual community spaces and new forms of mediated communications. This section deals with early attempts to make on-line communities more meaningful by limiting their membership to people who live in physical proximity to each other. These local communities represent exciting developments on the road to innovative and more powerful neighbourhoods for us all.

The first attempts were called freenets, also known as community networks. These on-line "clubs" have members who usually live in a particular city or town, and they provide useful information about that community's interests and activities. Members may visit the cyber equivalents of their schools, hospitals, town hall, post office, and so on. Often, they can "walk" through the town, stopping at the courthouse and government centre to discuss local issues with elected councillors, or at the medical arts building to discuss health issues with a medical professional. There are also bulletin boards, electronic mail, and other information services. Although these community networks vary in size, ideology, and governance, they all provide access to anyone who wishes to participate.

The information they provide is often similar to that provided by well-established non-electronic community networks that operate through workplaces, malls, sports and social clubs, schools, and churches. This kind of information can be found in the "What's Happening" pages of community newspapers, notices on laundromat walls, and city-hall leaflets delivered to households.

Community nets have been limited in their general appeal, however, by their self-selected membership of early adopters. Most of the nets were formed when less than 15 percent of community residents had on-line access. The demographics of these early adopter netizens showed that they tended to be higher-income, better-educated, technology-friendly males.

On the other hand, a small number of communities have approached connectivity from a universal access model. These twenty-first-century neighbourhoods provide the homes/apartments with digital connections to each other. I've coined the term "habicon" for this second type of connected community — from *habi*tat (the natural environment in which people live) and *con*nection. The emphasis here is on the location, the living environment, and the proximal relationship among the residents.

Habicons, although they appear superficially to be similar to community networks, have some distinguishing characteristics that enable their residents to have experiences that are different from those who join community nets. For example, although average community net subscribers have e-mail, it is unusual for them to correspond with each other or get together off-line. Residents in habicons, on the other hand, correspond on-line with their neighbours (both individually and as a group) because they know each other's e-mail addresses, thanks to the local e-directory, which promotes friendly communications and more face-to-face contacts within the community. They also get together for traditional community activities.

But before we look at habicons, let's examine the earlier community networks.

CHAPTER 7

Community Networks

IN 1999, ALMOST 200 NORTH AMERICAN COMMUNITIES WERE LISTED on the Internet Directory of Community Networks and Community Information Services. Most of these networks corresponded to cities or towns, although some, such as the Appalachian Center for Economic Networks (ACEnet), are linked to larger geographical regions. Their focus varies greatly.

For example, Blacksburg Electronic Village (BEV) in Virginia describes one of its strengths as follows: "We have a very active seniors group with more than 150 members. They have formed an active and vigorous social organization with many face-to-face meetings, social events, [and] training activities, . . . and [they] use e-mail and mailing lists to keep in touch with friends, family, and each other."

Canville Virtual Village, an on-line community in Westchester, Ohio, is unusual in that it is run as a for-profit organization. Its creators state, "We offer web page design and hosting services to individuals, small non-profit organizations, and small- to medium-sized businesses. We sell advertising on our BBS, on the website and in our newsletter."

The Northern California Indian Development Council, on the other hand, is a community network whose membership consists of eighteen American Indian communities in Northern California. They believe their on-line activities should extend the services they began offering in 1976 at the Indian Educational Center. Three

Rivers Free-Net, meanwhile, helps low-income single parents complete their education by offering links to free childcare, support counselling, and classes in parenting skills.

Freenets Evolve

To better understand the philosophy that underlies community networks such as those just described, let's first have a look at a brief history of the freenet movement. I am grateful to Donald Gutstein for his excellent book *e.con: How the Internet Undermines Democracy*, from which some of the information that follows is drawn.

The freenet movement really began in 1984, with Tom Grundner of Case Western Reserve University in Cleveland. While he was working on a medical-information system, Grundner came up with the idea of having members pose health questions on-line rather than making a visit to a clinic. He included this function in his software and arranged for a health professional to answer questions within twenty-four hours. The service was able to attract funding from AT&T and Ohio Bell, and it proved to be so popular that it was given its own nickname — St. Silicon's Hospital.

Within a few years, Grundner was able to take the concept and free it from its medical roots. Focused now on general community issues, he worked with the university to develop the first freenet. In 1986, the Cleveland freenet went into operation combining a local information system with personal e-mail accounts. The service had soon attracted 7,000 registered users, logging more than 500 calls a day by the end of that year.

Grundner decided to franchise the idea to encourage others to replicate Cleveland's success. He set up the National Public Telecomputing Network (NPTN), and took the position that any organization calling itself a freenet should conform to basic standards of service. But even in the mid-eighties, national borders led to problems with digital networks, which consider all users to be alike. Canadian networks were treated like their American counterparts, for example, and were required by NPTN to carry information about American presidents and the U.S. constitution. To counter this, Canadian community networks eventually established Telecommunities Canada, their own alternative umbrella organization, to deal with Canadian content and to break away from what they perceived as unnecessary central control. Unfortunately, Telecommunities Canada — which charged no licence fees — had limited funds and hence limited influence.

A more successful venture was the Canadian government's Community Access Program (CAP). Launched in 1994 by Industry Canada, CAP was able to kick-start community connections and network services in areas not well served by Internet service providers (ISPs). It has established more than 4,200 community sites in approximately 3,000 rural and remote areas of Canada, and has effectively become a competitor to Telecommunities Canada.

Many more community networks were formed in the mid-1990s, the result of individuals and organizations ramping up the information highway and assisting others in establishing on-line community relationships. The goal of these networks has been to encourage local community activities and provide information to residents about municipal, provincial, state, and federal government programs. These early freenets predated the 1992 advent of the Web and its browsers, so members had to use special communications software to connect.

Freenets tend to be concerned with local political issues and community action, activities that are not normally be supported by commercial advertisers. In 1994, the Free-Net Association in Victoria, B.C., sponsored a Free-Net Strategic and Marketing Plan, which explained that "Community Free-Nets view themselves as local public services operating under a model similar to public libraries or public broadcasting systems."

In his book, Gutstein argues that community networks should provide alternatives to commercialization. Indeed, he sees community networks as a mechanism for citizen empowerment, an opportunity for ordinary people, who might not otherwise have access to lobby groups, to reach and influence politicians.

Gutstein is not alone in his beliefs. The Association for Progressive Communications (APC) was founded in 1984 to serve the needs of the peace, human-rights, and social-justice movements. It began its on-line operations in 1990, and claims to have influenced many important world events, including the following:

- After the crackdown in Tiananmen Square in Beijing in 1989, student protesters used APC bulletin boards and e-mail lists to make available information that had been censored from the world's press. The Chinese government, desperate to stop the flow of embarrassing reports, tried to cut telephone links to the outside world.
- During the attempted Soviet coup in 1990, APC partners routed their on-line news stories through telephone networks in the Baltic states, then to Scandinavia, and from there to London and on to the rest of the world.
- More recently, the Zapatista rebels of southern Mexico were able to use the new media to focus the world's attention on their social struggle. By taking advantage of their Internet links with world media and non-governmental organizations, the Zapatistas were able to raise global awareness of their underfunded and under-manned campaign.
- The Multilateral Agreement on Investment (MAI), which Gutstein calls "a charter of rights for global capital," was a pet project for many of the world's leading politicians. Because the agreement included provisions that would compromise the cultural and economic sovereignty of individual states, these politicians hoped to push it through in relative obscurity. But U.S. consumer advocate Ralph Nader put a draft of the MAI on one of his web sites, and within days dozens of other groups in scores of countries had picked it up and started spreading the news. The power of e-mail lists quickly became evident: 600 groups in seventy countries signed on to oppose the agreement, which was eventually shelved (at least for the time being).

Some believe that connected communities can lead twenty-first-century citizens to counter powerful multinational-inspired, anti-democratic trends. But others think that they should focus on social issues and steer clear of corporate bashing. Doug Schuler, in his book *New Community Networks: Wired for Change*, notes, "Computer networks cannot . . . foment resistance to corporate control, but they can assist groups already working for social change." At the high point in Canada in 1996, there were thirty-five operating networks, with about 500,000 members, according to community network activists Garth Graham and Leslie Regan Shade. These spanned the country, from Halifax to Victoria to the Northwest Territories.

The success of the Internet and its World Wide Web has enabled almost all of these community nets to migrate to the larger public Internet, which allows netizens to visit their sites from anywhere in the world. The effect has been profound and, in many cases, harmful to the freenet movement. Once a community net moves to the Web, the people running it are encouraged to stop looking inward at their local community and to begin looking outward, a change in focus that often has these sights morphing into promotional chambers of e-commerce.

As a result, the line has blurred between true freenets and the promotional web sites that every town, city, region, province, state, and country now has. The latter are aimed at outside viewers, and are used to encourage tourism; attract businesses to the region; and provide information about local flora, fauna, demographics, and attractions. The community nets that have remained relevant have usually done so by collaborating with local governments to create even-handed access to information and discussions about current issues.

Minnesota Experiences

One of the most interesting community nets that was able to move to the web and still resist commercialization is the Minnesota E-Democracy forum, which has stayed true to its freenet roots as a political forum. It became a tax-exempt non-profit organization in 1996, and has as its mission to "improve participation in democracy in Minnesota through information networks."

Steven Clift, the chairman of the board, has been involved in the on-line democracy movement since 1993, when he started the Public Policy Network. In "Democracy Is Online," a 1998 article in the Internet Society's *On the Internet* magazine, he stated that "many people look at the crisis in politics as a disconnect between the government and the citizens. My view is that citizens are fundamentally disconnected from one another and hyper-connected to government through various special interest groups, [but that the Internet allows citizens to connect directly with each other]. . . . How often do legislative or parliamentary web sites encourage you to interact with other visitors interested in the same content or draft legislation?"

He continues, "Rarely do citizens connect with each other online within the context of local democracy. The fact that [politicians] represent geographic areas puts the nature of participation in democracy at odds with the technical ethos of the Internet, [which is global]. With so many [Internet users] hoping to escape the 'accident of geography,' how will those who want to use the Internet to 'come home' become connected with each other for civic purposes?"

Clift strikes at the heart of the issue of "local versus global" relevance. How do we combine our need to articulate and act on matters of local significance with the larger and increasingly important global culture? This will become a strong focus of attention as the world becomes more connected and people become increasingly concerned about losing their local cultures and control over their communities. The subject brings to mind a personal story whose punchline articulates a solution in a colourful manner.

In 1981, I was elected to my first highly visible public position: president of the Academy of Canadian Cinema. In that capacity, I had a dinner engagement with an influential entertainment lawyer, Michael Levine. Levine had made the reservation at a posh restaurant where the political and industrial elite supped.

At the time, I was a working film composer, fiercely proud of my artistic roots and determined not to let my new position diminish my individualistic and non-corporate image. Alas, the restaurant's maître d' did not share my ideological bent. When Levine arrived and we tried to enter the dining room, he barred me because I was not wearing a tie (or a dinner jacket, for that matter).

I was at a temporary loss for words when my friend whispered in the gatekeeper's ear and slipped him a bill, the denomination of which I was unable to ascertain. With a sweeping gesture, we were quickly ushered into the dining room, to a dark corner table far from the seats where the well known came to see and be seen.

After we had been seated, Levine waited a beat, then looked me in the eyes and said, "Let me give you some advice, Paul. If you want to find a balance between your personal culture and your need to influence others, think Yiddish, but dress British." When it's applied to the challenge of our age, this pearl of wisdom translates to "Adopt global wrappings to take advantage of online opportunities, but do so to serve your local interests."

Steven Clift came to the same conclusion in Minnesota. He decided to use his experience with the statewide forum to take the state web site local, to his home city. In the summer of 1998 he launched the Minneapolis Issues Forum (MPLS-ISSUES). Discussions focus on issues that residents want addressed by the city council, the local school board, and other Minneapolis boards and councils. These groups, in turn, are encouraged to make their meeting announcements, agendas, and information resources available online.

Clift's dream is that, as a result of the local web site, a discussion at the corner coffee shop might one day start like this: "You know, I missed that neighbourhood meeting on traffic calming the other day, but the e-mail discussion brought me up to date. I'll be at the next in-person meeting when they take that vote."

The Minneapolis site has influenced politicians on issues as mundane as dealing with an unusually high population of squirrels. But these kinds of sites can also have a national impact. Minnesota made national headlines when a former professional wrestler, Jesse Ventura, was elected governor. Phil Madsen, the on-line coordinator for Ventura's successful campaign, revealed that secret of his electoral success: "Could Jesse Ventura have won this election without his use of the Internet? . . . I say unequivocally no. For the first time the strategic use of the Internet . . . was required to win."

Balancing Commerce and Community

Just as many of the original freenets have added promotional activities (and hence support dollars from local governments and companies), some promotional web sites have added community information, weather reports, and discussion groups that are aimed at local residents.

Carl Knipfel, manager of marketing for Toronto's economic development and tourism departments, echoes the problem of mounting a city web site that tries to be everything to everyone. "My job is to make certain that someone looking for information to help them decide to visit or locate in Toronto can get what they want without being distracted by web site information they are not interested in. For them, the information that appeals to locals is just clutter. If they don't find what they are looking for in a few seconds, they click to another city."

Knipfel is speaking of the home page that most web site owners hope will become a portal to many streams of information and commerce relating to the site's focus. In the case of a city like Toronto, the home page contains links to movie listings, newspapers, magazines, radio and television guides, and restaurants. While these are useful for Torontonians, they may make it difficult for outsiders to find the business or tourism information they are seeking.

Knipfel's remarks make it clear that there is a huge gulf between the objectives of classic community freenets and community web sites sponsored by city and town councils. In fact, the former are aimed at individuals who wish to influence the politicians who preside over the latter.

Not surprisingly, there is a fundamental tension between freenet/ community networks as incubators of political action and government-supported programs that aim to provide universal Internet and information access to all communities. This tension may be resolved as community nets move to their next phase of development, as habicons. By definition, habicons provide on-line access to everyone within a neighbourhood, and must be cautious about promoting any particular political perspective. This will overcome a community net stereotype of a small group of ideologues lobbying for their particular political agendas.

Community Nets Falter

In general, community networks have not become the instruments for social change that their organizers hoped they would. Although they played an important role in getting early adopters to gather by geographic location, they failed to create a critical mass of public, non-profit community content that could compete with the richness and friendliness of the Web.

The content on community sites was frequently created with government grants. But when the grants ran out, the freenets were generally unable to mobilize volunteer forces to update their content and create new applications that would retain the interest of their existing members and attract new ones. Without a funding base for site and content maintenance, the freenets have been struggling to preserve and improve their relevance.

Perhaps the most important reason that community networks did not mature into ubiquitous vehicles for twenty-first-century democratic expression is that they were co-opted by the Internet, which has itself been overrun by the commercial forces that are anathema to freenets. As I detailed in *The Bagel Effect*, the driving forces at the close of the twentieth century were free markets and free enterprise, both of which have been expressed on the Web in the form of rampant advertising and consumer transactions. Since advertising and transactions are the economic engines that are driving the Internet and its offshoots, we should not expect community networks, which don't accept ads or allow commercial transactions, to thrive unless they are supported by tax dollars.

Thankfully, there are some community nets that have been successful. One is in Canada's Far North.

CHAPTER 8

Rankin Inlet: A Community Net

THE INUIT PEOPLE HAVE BEEN BUILDING STONE CAIRNS FOR thousands of years. The word for these in the Inuktitut language is Inukshuk (ee-nook-shook), which means "to look like a person [an Inuk]." They are used by the Inuit to mark high points of land, good hunting and fishing spots, or the way home, and are a symbol of trust and reassurance in the vast emptiness of the Arctic. William Belsey chose the Inukshuk as the symbol for his web site's home page after spending twenty years in the Arctic, living with and teaching Inuit children and elders using computers and later the Internet to connect them to the outside world and to each other.

They need it. The community of Rankin Inlet, where he taught, is more than one thousand kilometres from any other populated community. There are no roads or rails in or out, only airplanes that land when the weather permits, bringing in high-cost (because of the transportation expense) items to a place with little opportunity for people to earn a wage.

Belsey first learned about the Arctic from his Inuit brother-in-law, Michael Kusugak, an author of children's books. He was so fascinated by stories of the Arctic that when he first met Helene (later to become his wife), he told her, "If this relationship works out, I want you to know that I have always wanted to go to the North." She had no idea just how far north Belsey wanted to go, but when they graduated from Queen's University in Kingston, Ontario, in the early 1980s, she found out. Belsey was able to find a pair of job offers for both of them.

Because basics such as food are so expensive in the Far North, they were each given a salary advance of $1,000 to purchase essentials. Instead of doing that, Belsey blew the money on a computer. He had been influenced by one of his professors, Bill Higgenson, who had recently returned from working with MIT's Seymour Papert, creator of the children's computer language LOGO. At that time, the use of computers in education was almost unheard of, the domain of a few quirky hobbyist teachers.

Belsey remembers, "We took our food money and purchased a Texas Instruments TI-99 computer, as we could not afford an Apple, and these were the only machines that could run LOGO then. At the time, Helene and I owed over $20,000 in student loans, at 22 percent interest!"

In 1983, he began teaching in what was then Canada's Northwest Territories and is now a self-governing territory called Nunavut. This region is vast, peopled with hardy indigenous folk whose culture has been all but wiped out by the descendants of European explorers and immigrants and modern technology such as the rifle and snowmobile. But Belsey felt certain that the new technology of computers could have a reverse effect, and would encourage the preservation of local language and stories.

In the early 1990s, Belsey was the leading force in establishing a local bilingual (English and Inuktitut) community network, which he believes can bring the best of the outside world into the community while preserving and promoting its local culture and connecting its residents to their kin throughout the Arctic.

By 1994, Belsey drafted a computer purchase plan for the Keewatin Divisional Board of Education and was able to raise more than $100,000 from government and corporations to implement it. This was no small feat in a community of 2,000, 80 percent of whom are Inuit whose closest previous exposure to high tech had been snowmobiles. He worked with Sakku Arctic Investments, the corporation charged with the responsibility of investing Nunavut land-claims money on behalf of the Inuit beneficiaries. They created an Internet service and made it available to all residents, even those who didn't have computer skills or lacked the financial resources to pay for the service.

When Belsey made his case to the local education council, he showed the members a virtual on-line tour of the Louvre in Paris. Lucien Taparti, an influential elder who had recently survived a polar bear attack, was now staring at Vincent Van Gogh's *Starry Night* on a computer screen. "He saw the potential for kids in the community," says Belsey.

On October 28, 1996, a press release proclaimed:

> *Rankin Inlet proudly welcomes everyone to the grand opening of the Northwest Territories' very first Community Access Centre on Saturday November 2nd at 2:00 p.m. in the computer room of Leo Ussak Elementary School. The center, known as Igalaaq, Inuktitut for window, will be a technological window to the world for the citizens of Rankin Inlet. . . . To date over $80,000 in goods, services and cash has been generated in only one year!*

A reporter for the *Ottawa Citizen* covered the event, and quoted Aaron Forbes, a seventeen-year-old student volunteer at Igalaaq, as saying, "It gives people a chance to see what the outside world is like, aside from TV. On TV, you can only get what's given to you, but on the Internet, you can get everything."

The *Citizen* article continued: "This night, –30°C with a vicious wind from the north, Igalaaq is so crowded that volunteers enforced half-hour limits at the 17 terminals. William Tiktak, 11, types a conversation with two boys in distant Yellowknife. Inukshuk Aksalnik, 16, gathers information on Marie Antoinette for her project on the French Revolution. Nearby, insulated by headphones and oblivious to his surroundings, a boy downloads the music of bluesman Stevie Ray Vaughn."

It didn't take long before residents were reaching out to people all over the world. The following e-conversation was taken from the web site of the Leo Ussak Elementary School. It's a conversation between Evan, a grade four student, and an unnamed student somewhere else in the world who is curious about what it's like to live in the Arctic. The conversation is in English, a second language for kids in Rankin Inlet.

> I will answer your questions.
> *Do you eat musk ox?*
> I never eat musk ox.
> *What do you eat most of?*
> Tuktuk [caribou] is the easiest animal to hunt. They are bigger and fatter.
> *What do you eat at Thanksgiving?*
> At Thanksgiving we eat turkey, stuffing, tuktuk, apple and lemon pie.
> *What do most Inuit eat?*
> Most Inuit eat tuktuk, seal, polar bear, rabbit, ptarmigan and tea.
> *What is your favorite desert?*
> I eat cheesecake, banana bread and ice-cream.

The above conversation encapsulates the dichotomy between globalization, which imposes the world's most popular languages and cultures on previously isolated communities, and localization, which nurtures the differentiated needs and cultures of these same communities. Unlike the mass media, community nets are symmetrical and allow locals to contribute their uniqueness in addition to absorbing the larger uniformity.

The community net has focused on issues and events that are meaningful to locals, such as the Julie Hansen International Arctic Expedition, which travelled by dog team from Churchill, Manitoba, to Tuktuyaktuk, Northwest Territories, while students in Rankin Inlet tracked its progress on their web site using information from a global positioning satellite. By focusing on events with strong local interest and involving a large number of community members, Belsey was able to plant the seeds of community ownership, thus encouraging ordinary townsfolk to make the network their own.

Belsey left the Arctic in June 1998, and he has been writing and speaking on the topic of community networks since then. I ran into him at a conference last year and asked him the question that was foremost in my mind: "What has happened to the community network since you left?" The question was pertinent because, in the course of researching this book, I had followed dozens of community network efforts around the world and had found, to my dismay, that most of them faltered after the initial organizer left the helm or the external funding ran out.

Belsey answered, "It has only become stronger. We planted some very hardy seeds that have taken root quite well in the tundra soil!" I checked this myself by logging onto the Rankin Inlet web sites, and I was pleased to note that, indeed, this on-line community is thriving. I was especially taken with the elementary school's web site and its list of objectives for its information technology programs.

> *Students will use Information Technology (I-T) to:*
> * *preserve Inuit culture;*
> * *bridge the gap between youth and elders;*
> * *gain employment skills;*
> * *improve community participation in the educational system;*
> * *use the school to offer opportunities for economic development and community wellness;*
> * *stimulate interest in lifelong learning and encourage school attendance.*

In July 1997, Belsey was asked to be a founding member of 2B1, a foundation that strives to bring information technology and Internet access to remote parts of the world. Other founding members were Nicholas Negroponte and Seymour Papert, of MIT's Media Lab. At that time, Belsey was able to share his story directly with Papert, whose original work unknowingly inspired his entire cyber-journey.

CHAPTER 9

Stonehaven West: A Habicon

W E MOVE FROM RANKIN INLET, THE TINY COMMUNITY IN the middle of nowhere, to the exurban town of Newmarket, thirty kilometres north of Toronto, a megacity with a population of 4 million. In 1996, the Stonehaven West neighbourhood development was connected by a high-speed intranet as part of a $100-million trial of a wired community. This is the experiment referred to in Part One.

As so often happens in these cases, this community was selected by chance. In 1992, CulTech, my research centre at York University, had undertaken Cities of the Future, a modest project funded by the federal government to investigate the potential impacts of digital connectivity on urban design. The following year, U.S. Vice-President Al Gore, aided and abetted by Wall Street hype, coined the term "information superhighway" as a metaphor for the impact that digital networks would have on all aspects of twenty-first-century living. The idea was simple to grasp. Just as the American interstate highway system championed by Gore's father had connected the country for moving goods, services, and people across the land, so would the new information highway system criss-cross the country to move information products across the land. The result would be greatly increased commerce and productivity, a better quality of life, and a vindication of the American way of life as the global model of progress.

I changed the name of our research project to Cities on the Information Highway and immediately began to get interest from governments, corporations, and the media, all of which wanted to learn about and be part of this exciting new form of communication that was about to sweep the land. In the early 1990s, most pundits were predicting that this connectivity and information change would take place with television sets, because they were ubiquitous, as opposed to personal computers, which had very low consumer penetration (less than 10 percent at the time).

If television sets were to be the appliance of choice, then surely movies-on-demand would be the content of choice, since focus groups indicated that viewers would love to choose their movies and control the times they could watch them. Movies-on-demand trial announcements popped up frequently, but the cost of these (in the hundreds of million dollars), were a barrier to all but a few large corporations that had direct strategic interests at stake — entertainment conglomerates, telephone companies (telcos), and cable-television companies (cablecos).

I knew that to mount a significant trial, I would have to interest some large companies in participating. My opportunity arose when I helped organize a conference on multimedia and networking in Banff, Alberta. I met Sudhir Joshi, a marketer for IBM's broadband network products who was also on the committee, and told him about CulTech's connected cities project. He told me that, at one of its California research labs, IBM had recently developed a video server that could deliver movies-on-demand over a fibre-optic network, and that the company had decided to test it in Toronto. (Toronto was chosen because Canada has the highest penetration of cable TV in the world and the city offered the most up-to-date fibre-optic network available at the time.)

The trial was to take place between an engineering facility of Rogers Cablevision and the downtown campus of Rogers Communications Centre, at Ryerson University. I was excited that my home city had been chosen as the site of an important test in my field of research, and I asked if there was any way my research centre could become involved. A few days later, Sudhir got back to me. This trial was technical in nature, he explained, and was intended to see if the equipment would work over a long fibre-distribution route. But the equipment could be made available for ongoing research if someone could arrange a trial with consumers who would use the system and evaluate its desirability.

I left that meeting feeling very excited and determined to find a way to make Toronto a trial centre for this type of activity. The stumbling block was finding a willing and unbiased group of consumer participants. I mulled the problem for several weeks with my associate director, Dr. Jerome Durlak, an expert in communications policy and community living. We both agreed that the easiest route would be to find a real-estate developer with a subdivision project in progress and convince him to make it part of our trial. Our research results would provide important information that would give the developer a leg up on his competitors, since new neighbourhoods would increasingly be built with a communications infrastructure in place.

As is the case with many important projects, this one started with a few hiccups. The first developer I approached was very enthusiastic but, after several months of discussion, passed on the opportunity because I insisted that the trial needed to connect *all* the residents within a neighbourhood. He felt that the new services should be profit-driven, which implied that only affluent early adopters would participate.

Back to square one. Everywhere I went, I mentioned that I was interested in connected communities. After a few weeks, Virginia Solomon, an architect friend, told me I should visit her husband's cousin Carey Solomon, a real-estate developer whose hobby was computers. When I visited Solomon at his office, it was clear that we were on the same wavelength. Instead of having to be sold on the idea, he spent the meeting trying to convince *me* that such a trial was necessary.

Solomon's company was building a community in Newmarket that was partially through the approval process, and he was willing to make it available for the trial and to make some contributions towards the infrastructure costs. I set up a meeting with Solomon, Sudhir Joshi from IBM, and Daryll Williams, who was then director of the Rogers Communications Centre. Bingo! At that meeting, we were all finishing one another's sentences. We all agreed that the trial should be non-profit and consortium-based, and that it should allow a very wide range of participants, including competitors. We agreed that the timing was "pre-competitive," meaning that the general commercial use of our trial content would be several years down the road. Therefore, competitors could work together so that all would better understand the opportunities and mechanisms for ultimately making money in the new sector. It seemed that everyone involved would benefit from finding out what sort of content users might like. After the killer applications were found (there seemed no doubt that this would happen), all participants would move into competition phase for their piece of the pie.

We named the trial Intercom Ontario, after the connection technology developed in the 1940s (intercoms) and our expectation (mistaken, as it turned out) that the Ontario government would provide significant funding. We spread the word, and almost immediately I was swamped with calls from companies and organizations that wanted to participate. We felt that unlike the American information highway trials, which were exclusive to a few large partners, our trial should include many companies, including start-ups and software providers. This, we believed, would add significant pieces to the complex puzzle of delivering value to on-line consumers.

And our puzzle was much more complex than those in other trials. Time-Warner's trial in Orlando, Florida, was the international benchmark, with the highest cost (about $1 billion Canadian) and the most publicity. That trial involved only a few companies delivering Warner movies to Silicon Graphics computers (disguised as set-top boxes). The computers were connected to television sets, with home shopping thrown in for good measure.

We aimed much higher and approached the test from a different perspective. My research centre had already developed a framework for evaluating technology change and predicting the future of digital connectivity (this was the Bagel Effect I later wrote about). In its stripped-down form, our guiding principle was simple to apply. *Control and power are moving from suppliers to consumers. Focus on the end-users, and you will arrive at a correct conclusion.* The simplicity was disarming, but the correctness of predictions was astonishing.

In this case, applying the Bagel Effect gave us the following guidelines for the trial:

- Forget movies-on-demand. Even though pundits were all predicting that this would be the killer app, it offered viewers nothing
new. To be sure, they would be able to watch a movie on a television set, fast forward and rewind, and pause for pee breaks and tea
breaks. But they could already do this by renting a movie from
their local video shop. And while the video shop charged two
dollars for a rental, the most optimistic estimates of the cost of
delivering a movie over a broadband network at that time was
about five dollars. So where's the beef? We decided not to invest
any time, money, or technical resources in movies-on-demand
(even though this had been the driving technology when we incu-
bated the trial). Subsequently, all the movie-on-demand trials,
including Time-Warner's, fizzled for lack of viewer interest at the
proposed price points.
- Forget using set-top boxes and televisions — use computers
instead. Here we were going out on a limb because, in 1994, the
penetration of home computers was so low that corporate planners
could not make a business case for deploying an expensive network
to service them. The rationale, however, was clear: to perform the
needed functions, a set-top box would need to be a powerful computer, albeit one stripped down without disk drives or add-on slots.
(Time-Warner came to the same conclusion when it decided to
partner with Silicon Graphics.)

   But if you need a set-top to make your TV receive digital
information, then you need one for each TV in the house, like
cable boxes today. And if the cost of a single TV set-top was considered much too expensive (more than $500 at the time), the cost of
multiple set-tops for each TV would be prohibitive. On the other
hand, computer technology would allow a single unit to act as a
server for an entire home, distributing different content to different
rooms simultaneously. Most important, a computer is inherently an
interactive device that has evolved with keyboards, mice, and other
input devices that are difficult to integrate into a television environment. These were needed to enable users to control their content
and scheduling.

   These conclusions were obvious to all of us who were toying

with a newfangled software application called an Internet browser, which made it incredibly simple to provide and access multimedia content on a subset of the Internet that had been dubbed the World Wide Web. A computer connected to the Web really put the user in charge of the activity, a classic Bagel Effect technology.

We therefore decided to go with computers as the user appliance of choice while others, particularly the cablecos in their trials, went with television sets. The difference was again clear: we were looking at the service from the user's perspective while most others were looking at it from their corporate perspective. And in the end, the television-based trials failed while the success of the World Wide Web caused computer sales to shoot through the roof.

Finally, we held the heretical notion that instead of designing the content from the perspective of solid business cases, we should present users with a great variety of applications that might be of interest to them, including community services, education, and information — applications that every focus group told us would be most desirable for consumers but that had no viable business models at that time.

A great advantage of driving a project that many others want to participate in is that you can maintain your agenda even though it may not closely match the corporate strategy of your participants. We were able to convince large companies to briefly sublimate their corporate strategies in order to find out what their customers wanted. The following is an extract from the trial's membership recruiting materials:

> *The neighbourhood is a test bed to gauge user reaction to networked content, applications, and appliances. Personal communications, entertainment, educational materials, information, community activities, health, and other content will be delivered on demand. Research will focus on changes in work, play, and family activities in the wired community. . . .*
>
> *The Intercom consortium structure allows many companies to participate [that] have been excluded from other trials that restrict participation to a few large industrially allied companies.*

Contributions from smaller and/or out-of-sector members may prove crucial to the trial's success.

Intercom Ontario also unites competitive organizations, which do not generally co-operate within their sector. It also mingles regulators and regulated businesses together in a pre-competitive experience to develop a common vocabulary and understanding of the opportunities and pitfalls ahead.

We were keen to find out how ordinary people would react in a connected environment. Would greater home-centredness be the result of consumers being able to do things with home appliances that previously required that they leave the home? If so, would that lead to fewer interpersonal contacts? Would residents use the community connections in their homes to facilitate local relationships? There was no consensus as to whether the connectivity would free up time that would otherwise be spent in transportation for relationships with neighbourhood residents.

By January 1995, we had been able to sign up almost eighty members for the consortium from a wide array of industries and government agencies, including museums, TV networks, multimedia organizations, newspapers, periodicals, academic institutions, and computer specialists, among others.

A Telco and a Cableco Get into Bed

There were quite a few competitors from each industrial sector (and more joined later), but we had only a few choices of telecommunications carriers, the folks who would connect the homes to each other and to our servers, some of which were fifty kilometres away from the site. Originally, we worked with the local cableco, Rogers Cablesystems. Although company representatives were enthusiastic, I found it difficult to get firm commitments from them on timetables, contributions, technologies, and other critical aspects of planning. Weeks went by, and I became concerned that if this lack of progress continued, we would not be able to meet the milestones of our proposed implementation.

I spoke with executives from Rogers Cablesystems and suggested they review our proposal and either endorse it or decline to do so by a fixed date. The date came and went with no answer. I let a two-day grace period elapse and then called Stu Verge, then vice-president of networks for Bell Canada.

Verge had appeared in an early fund-raising video for CulTech Research Centre, and he was sympathetic to our idea for an industry-wide pre-competitive trial with shared experiences and results. I explained my frustration with the lack of responsiveness from Rogers and asked him if Bell Canada would be interested in providing the bandwidth. Without missing a beat, he said, "Meet me at my office tomorrow afternoon and we'll have a substantive chat."

The next day, I went to the Bell Trinity Street headquarters and met with Verge and Bell's vice-president for broadband networks, Bob Campbell, who later became the first Intercom Ontario trial manager. They were both enthusiastic about Bell's participation and wanted to know if there were any special terms or conditions we would attach. "Just one," I said. "Rogers Cablesystems is already a consortium member, and if they wish to collaborate on supplying the network, you will have to work with them." Pause. Sharp intake of breath. Then, after a few moments of silence, Verge answered, "We can live with that for a pre-competitive trial."

The next day, I was feeling pretty good about the way things had gone until the telephone rang. It was Dave Masotti from Rogers Cablesystems. "Sorry it's taken us a while longer than expected, but the Rogers board has decided to go ahead with your consortium for the trial."

Pause at my end. Sharp intake of breath. Then I said, "We're very pleased to hear that, Dave, but since I hadn't heard from you as expected, I've already arranged for Bell to provide the network. . . . I did make it a condition of participation that Bell would have to collaborate with your company, since you had spoken with us first, but now, if you want to participate, you'll have to work with Bell."

Pause at Masotti's end. Sharp intake of breath. Then he said, "You understand I have to take this back to the board." Of course, I said. About a week later, Masotti called back to say that Rogers would agree to collaborate if we kept the joint participation under wraps (because the telecommunications giants were already at each other's throats in public and at the government's regulatory hearings).

So we kept mum, and for several months there were secret meetings at which Rogers and Bell met with our non-aligned technical people to discuss how we could construct a network that would mate the high-bandwidth cableco connections to the homes with the telco switching network.

The collaboration made too much sense to last. In the world of corporate competition, what's best for the consumer is less important than what's best for a corporation's overall strategic positioning. In this case, the public antagonism between the telecommunications competitors become too intense for our partnership to continue, so it fell apart.

Rogers left the consortium and Bell Canada ended up as our network supplier. The telco turned out to be a strong partner for us throughout the balance of the trial, but I always regretted losing the opportunity to use a breakthrough technology that combined the physical networks of cablecos and telcos and that could have influenced the worldwide dissemination of broadband content.

The Homeowners

Stonehaven West, the suburban neighbourhood where the Intercom Ontario trial took place, was a connected community in which almost all residents were on-line. The participants each made a commitment to participate (opted in) by signing an agreement that allowed us to monitor their actions and interactions on-line. In return, we undertook not to reveal any individual's on-line activities or sell any of their personal data to marketers.

The houses in Stonehaven West cost, on average, $200,000, and thus were considered "affordable" for the Toronto area. Most residents were first-time homeowners. A demographic study revealed that most buyers were young couples with one or two children, and that most had incomes and levels of education about 20 percent above the national average, about par for the area. They thought the trial would be valuable because it would give them access to education for their kids and for themselves. And while they couldn't quantify what

this "education" would be, they felt it would be increasingly important for everyone in the family.

To participate in our trial, each home owner was required to purchase certain equipment — a computer and a video camera (for about
$1,000) so that we would have a uniform platform for which to design
software. We would not have been able to tolerate the time and
expense needed to figure out how to get every sort of PC clone working with our advanced, memory-hungry, and processor-intensive
applications. Consortium members Apple Canada and Spectrum
Communities subsidized the equipment so that the price of entry was
not a significant barrier to use.

In fact, the trial was so intriguing and appealing that 85 percent of
the households signed up, perhaps the highest penetration of any
such trial in which participants were required to pay a fee. The percentage would have been even higher if not for the fact that a portion
of the homeowners were not fluent in English and didn't understand
our written solicitations. For all practical purposes, the entire community was on-line. Consequently, Stonehaven West qualified as a
habicon, one of the few indicators we have of what future communities will be like.

The Networks

There were two networks involved: the external community area
network (CAN) and the internal home area network (HAN). The external network was an intranet, or private network. Like AOL, @Home,
RoadRunner, or DSL, this intranet used Internet protocols and could
accommodate Internet browsers and content, but it maintained privacy with its firewalls (electronic filters that control the flow of digital
packets to and from the global Internet). Thus the neighbourhood
services and bulletin boards were private to the residents, and no one
logging onto the Internet from outside our trial could access these.

The speed of the network was very high, even by today's standards. Each home connection had a capacity of ten megabits per
second going in and out (i.e., symmetrical). The high speed of our
network and PCs meant that we could install decent-quality video
telephones for a hardware cost of only $100 per home. It also meant

that users could be content suppliers as well as content consumers. This feature became important in later stages of the trial, when we put residents on television rather than just having them watch it.

Our symmetrical network differed from the commercial high-speed networks that are being deployed today. Both the telcos and cablecos have opted for asymmetrical networks that can deliver much higher bandwidth downstream (from the service provider to the home) than upstream (from the home back to the service provider). This is based on the old assumption that Internet users, like television viewers, do not wish to create or send large amounts of data. I guess these network designers never heard *Star Trek*'s Captain Jean-Luc Picard say "onscreen" or considered the billions of home movies and home music recordings that users would like to share with their friends and relatives over the Net.

Our community area network technology was hybrid fibre-coax — that is, fibre-optic cables ran to each group of homes and then to a pod (a metal box) that converted the light signals to electronic signals, which then travelled over standard coaxial television-type cables to each individual home. At each home, Nortel, a consortium member, provided a personal computer conversion unit (PCCU) that accepted the mingled signals on the coaxial cable and split out the home telephone and on-line services. It could have distributed cable TV as well, but in 1996 Canadian telephone companies were not yet licensed to deliver those signals.

The HAN wiring in each home was installed by IBM using a combination of computer network cables (CAT 5), coaxial copper (TV type), and twisted copper pairs (like those used for your telephone). This wiring allowed residents to interconnect computers, television sets, telephones, and other electronic appliances in many rooms of the home. The cost was about $1,500 per home, and was absorbed by the real-estate developer, Spectrum Communities.

The on-line services travelled through the homes using the popular Ethernet protocol, which is employed today in most businesses and increasingly in homes. The wiring bundles terminated in wall outlet boxes — called drops — that were placed in areas throughout the home where users could plug in TVs, computers, telephones, and so on. Depending on its size, a home came with three to five of these drops installed. They were generally placed in the office, the play-room, and a bedroom or two. One of the earliest research results was that homebuyers were purchasing extra drops at $350 apiece so that they could access services in additional locations around the home. This was considered very significant, particularly by the developer, whose experience was that first-time homebuyers put every cent they have into the down payment and rarely opt for extra-cost items unless these have significant ongoing value (such as tile in the entrance hall).

Popular locations for extra drops were the kitchen, the bath-rooms, and additional bedrooms. But putting drops in kitchens was controversial at the time. All the builders we spoke to told us that kitchens were never considered large enough by residents, who always wanted more counter and cupboard space. Builders were cer-tain their customers would never sacrifice valuable kitchen real estate to a computer or television monitor.

Wrong! In 1999, I spoke with Monica Marics, director of the Broadband Innovation Group at AT&T's MediaOne Labs. She described research that her group had conducted with customers of her company's cable-modem service. At a presentation at an IBM-sponsored conference, she showed photographs of apartment and home kitchens laden with computers, televisions, and telephones, some in quarters so cramped that there was little room left for cook-ing or dining. Once again, users proved that, with new technology, they will rarely conform to the patterns expected by providers.

The Interface

Because we wanted to differentiate our services from television and computer programs, we designed a novel user interface — the graphic appearance of the desktop and its navigational underpinning. It was compatible with both computer and television monitors, but it didn't look or work like either one. Among other things, the user could nav-igate entirely by sound, a boon for the vision impaired. As the cursor moved over active buttons on the screen, unique musical sounds com-bined to form melodies and harmonies that could be used to indicate your screen position and menu level.

We wanted to stay away from the look and feel of an Internet browser or a computer operating system because research has shown that the complexity and clutter of these interfaces is a barrier for non-technical users and especially for the computer-challenged. Instead, we invented a system that never had more than seven graphic images on the screen at any time. Larger numbers of objects have been shown not to be individually resolved by the brain, and thus become a muddle to those not familiar with the images.

Here's how we limited the number of category images onscreen at any one time: rolling over an image that represents a category such as leisure, for example, erases the other images on the screen and brings up a new set of images that represent the sub-categories, such as games, music, and so on.

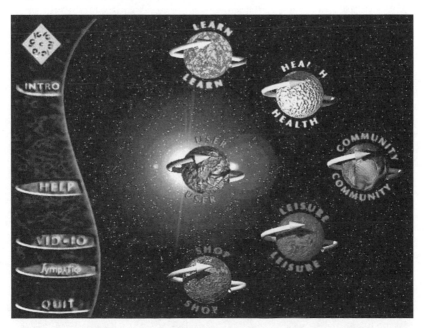

This figure illustrates the interface using planetary images for categories of content. You can access more than one thousand different applications and content with no more than two clicks of the mouse, with no menus on the screen and no folders to nest.

The Intercom interface was a big hit with first-time users. The jury at the international HIDE Awards (for user interfaces) in California said, "This is simply the finest example of hierarchy navigation ever. . . . It encourages exploration and things work just the way you would expect but with much less effort than normal." Yet after a year of use, many of our participants told us they would prefer an interface that would get them to their content destinations faster, even if it was less intuitive. They were less interested in browsing their options than they were in getting immediately to the few activities they did every day. This was particularly true of teenage boys, who would log on and immediately go to the same gaming web site every day.

We learned not only that different users like different interfaces, but also that individual users may prefer different interfaces as their familiarity with the system grows. An interface that is excellent for first-time users may no longer be best once they become power users. Consequently, we designed a second-generation interface that could accommodate several types of navigation, simply by analyzing the activities of a user and adjusting the mode of operation according to his or her measured proficiency. Unfortunately, the trial ended before we could deploy it.

About six months into the trial, I asked my staff who the heavy on-line users were. It turned out that our biggest user was a four-year-old girl. This information piqued my interest because a child at that age is not likely literate. Yet our interface required that users log in with their username and password. We wondered how she did it and sent a video crew to record the explanation.

It turned out that she had memorized the positions of the relevant computer keys, as well as the order in which they needed to be pressed. She explained her log-in system very articulately: "First you press this one, and then this one, and then this one, and then you must wait. . . . Then you press this one, then this one, and then you get to the game."

The little girl had learned to overcome the complexity of the log-in process and navigation techniques because her actions resulted in her getting to the on-line content she valued. In other words, her desire to reach a destination — a CD-ROM for kids with a game on it — helped her overcome the difficulty of learning a new system. She went to all the trouble of memorizing the keys on the computer keyboard just to get to that destination.

The lesson here is that people will go to a lot of trouble to overcome a complicated user interface if there is an activity or a service of value to them at the end of the process. On the other hand, if you provide connectivity without valuable activities, users will complain about the difficulty of using the interface no matter how well it is designed.

"Content rules!" as they say.

CHAPTER 10

A Friendlier Place to Live

A S I NOTED EARLIER, ONE OF THE FIRST AND MOST IMPORTANT research results to emerge from the Intercom trial was that residents told us their community was the friendliest one in which they had ever lived. They got to know more of their neighbours sooner through the simple community listserv.

In the Intercom Ontario neighbourhood, residents could communicate one to one (using e-mail) and also one to many (using the listserv). They also used their telephones and videophones. Interestingly, as was illustrated by the barbecue party mentioned in Part One, the neighbours who had access to the mediated communication also met more frequently face to face because they lived in the same physical community. As a matter of fact, we found that on-line connectivity had the effect of promoting in-person get-togethers, not the reverse. The experiences we monitored showed residents increasing their modes of communications, adding on-line text and video conversations to their normal social encounters.

Connectivity also had a notable effect on the democratic workings of the community and on the power flow to individual residents. For example, one resident noted that his lawn and driveway were unfinished although his contract with the developer stated they would be done by a certain date. Instead of dealing directly with the developer from a position of weakness, he posted an e-note asking if others had the same unfulfilled contractual arrangements. Within a few days, half the homeowners had agreed to meet and deal with their common problem. They decided to approach the developer jointly and electronically, and they threatened to petition the town council and stall the approval of the next phase of building until they had their lawns and driveways finished. The united homebuyers got much quicker action from the developer than a single complainant would have.

Residents also shared information about reliable auto-repair shops and neighbourhood retail stores that were having sales. They shared information about baby-sitters, garbage pick-ups, and used ice skates that their kids had outgrown. There were frequent postings about lost cats, dogs, and hamsters, and almost as frequent postings about found animals. When there was an attempted break-in at one home, the event was broadcast on-line throughout the neighbourhood along with an action plan for residents to jointly monitor each other's premises, particularly when a neighbour was not at home.

We found that the time residents spent on-line was generally cannibalized from television watching, not from going out to movies or socializing. The reduced television time that we witnessed is consistent with video-game research, which shows that kids who play home video games or surf the Internet watch much less television.

From day one, the trial participants wanted their homes to be wired to each other, not only to the Internet. "That," said a member of the Sauer family, "has been a very different experience. "We haven't been in the neighbourhood very long, but I found that we have gotten to know people much quicker than I think we would have. . . . It's really quite amazing. . . . It's made us a closer community."

The residents' assertion that Stonehaven West was the friendliest community they had ever lived in was echoed in a connected community trial far away — in London, England. In the 1998 MSNStreet trial, run by Microsoft, sixty participants in twenty-four households formed a wired community neighbourhood. Each household was given a computer, a modem, an Internet account (with MSN), a dedicated telephone line, a selection of software, a contribution towards telephone bills, and on-site installation and tutoring by specialists. Microsoft set up a private web site, a bulletin board, and a dedicated telephone help line. In return for this all-expenses-paid connection to the

Internet, participants had to keep a logbook of their on-line activities.

In a 1998 article for the *New York Times* on the Web, Bruno Gius-sani noted that for many, the MSNStreet project provided a substitute for the classic ice-breaker of asking your neighbour for a cup of sugar. Pearson Phillips, a retired journalist living there, said, "I used to know maybe five or six people in the street. Now I know at least forty of them quite well, and some very closely." As he scrolls through dozens of messages posted on the bulletin board, Phillips explains how the participants have been able to exchange information like gardening tips, recommend a decent plumber, find a trustworthy baby-sitter, or swap notes on local shops and restaurants.

"Kids have been asking for help with homework, others have posted messages looking for somebody to receive a parcel or to feed the cat," he said. "This creates a stronger feeling of participating in a community that cares about its members." The shared experience of being neophyte netizens and the ability to discuss local issues on the bulletin board "has meant that when we meet face to face we can carry on discussions instead of blandly talking about the weather," adds another participant, Jane Judd.

Peter McCartney, one of the participants, believes the most important impact was that the street's residents became closer socially. "There has been a significant improvement in communication [among us] in the street which would not have happened otherwise." Indeed, many things can prevent neighbours from getting to know one another, especially in a residential street full of lawyers, journalists, and other professionals who head downtown early in the morning and aren't back until dusk.

Common-interest discussions have also taken place on-line. Residents debated a proposed municipal plan that was to introduce controlled parking on nearby streets, a plan that had created concerns that their street would be flooded by cars. The bulletin board has also been used to gain support for a campaign against disruptive vibrations caused by the local railway. And when a burglar struck on the street, the news was circulated immediately, prompting a discussion about whether the street needed better lighting.

"There is no doubt that . . . for all the talk of wiping out time zones and geographical distances, e-mail will become the normal way to exchange local information," says Andrew Graham, an Oxford professor who monitored the project.

The Stonehaven West Listserv

The following messages were taken from the daily listserv correspondence of Stonehaven residents. Readers who are familiar with virtual on-line communities will notice how much this one differs because these folks live near each other, know each other socially (or want to), can meet to exchange items, and so on. The level of trust is significantly higher for these residents, who cannot "spoof" each other because there are no pseudonyms to hide behind.

Taken in their totality, the messages paint a better picture of a habicon than I can do with words. I have removed the names of the residents, which appeared in all the original messages. There are no pseudonyms or "handles" in the actual messages.

———————————————

Date: Sun., 4 May 1997
Subject: House Warming/Open House

You are cordially invited to a house warming/open house 10 May 97 from 6.00 PM on. Drop in for a few minutes or drop in for the night we would be pleased to see you. I will provide food please bring your own refreshments.

———————————————

Date: Mon., 28 July 1997

The Festival Wind Orchestra, a community band based a little south of Newmarket, is looking for some additional dedicated musicians to fill in some empty chairs. There are no audition requirements other than the ability to fog a cold mirror with your breath and even that can be waived if you play percussion instruments. Of course it would be helpful if you can read music, own an instrument and have some past experience playing in an ensemble.

Date: Fri., 29 Aug. 1997
Subject: Mosport Festival tickets

I have 16 $58 general admission tickets to this weekend's festival at Mosport. If You want to go you can call me after 2.00pm today. Good for today tomorrow and Sunday.

They are FREE.

Date: Wed., 3 Sept. 1997

I am looking to hire a cleaning lady to help around the house. If anyone in the neighborhood knows of someone reliable and trustworthy, please let me know either via e-mail or telephone. Thank you.

Date: Sun., 7 Sept. 1997

Does anyone have a recipe for Butter Tart Squares? I need it by Wednesday.

Date: Mon., 22 Sept. 1997
Subject: Special municipal meeting
Purpose: To consider zoning plans proposed by [the developer] regarding lands to the North of the School.

I have just learned that a special planning meeting to revue a proposal for new homes on the lands just North of the school will be held tomorrow evening. With the immediate past history of the Stonehaven West Development in mind, I have some serious reservations about the desirability of this new project going ahead while our existing problems appear to be dragging on.

I have been advised by our Regional Councilor that this meeting is open to the public and a space on the agenda will be made available to anybody who wants to go on record as having some input.

Date: Mon., 6 Oct. 1997

Hi my name is X and i am selling Magic cards i have about 100 cards and i am 12 years old.

Date: Tues., 7 Oct. 1997
Subject: I NEED FRIENDS

Hi everybody,
My name is Y and i am looking for kids in between the age 8-12. If you know enybod please E-mail me.

Date: Mon., Oct. 20, 1997

I AM DOING A SURVAY ON TYPES OF MUSIC PEOPLE LISTEN TO (THIS IS FOR SCHOOL) YOUR CHOICES ARE: R&B\RAP, ROCK, ALTERNATIVE, HEAVY METAL, OTHER

Date: Fri., 31 Oct. 1997

As a teacher in the secondary system in your community, I feel that it is important to share my knowledge of the impact of the changes proposed under Bill 160. If you are a parent, a grandparent, an aunt/uncle, or a citizen, or a student with concern for the future of education and our students, I urge you to take in as much information as possible about this Bill. I recognize the need for educational reform, but after reading the Bill, I fail to see how some of the major changes will benefit our children.

_____

Date: Sun., 9 Nov. 1997

IF ANYONE SEES A BLACK CAT WANDERING AROUND COULD
YOU PLEASE CALL [phone number]. HE ANSWERS TO THE NAME
OF TOBY, AND RAN AWAY AROUND 4:30PM.

_____

Date: Sun., 16 Nov. 1997

My grade 12 English students are preparing to send gift boxes to other
teenagers in 3rd World countries.

We need shoeboxes, specifically ones with lids, to pack the gifts in. If
you have any to give, please email me or call and I will come and pick
them up.

_____

Date: Mon., 24 Nov. 1997

You asked about the "Stonehaven Community Association" General
Meeting tonight, and "if any one attended I'd love to know what was
discussed." Well, I attended along with about 40 others, and here's
some notes:
Meeting Topics:
#1 Outdoor Ice Rink
#2 Rezoning the Land North of Stonehaven Elementary School
Etc.

_____

Date: Sun., 7 Dec. 1997

HAPPY HOLIDAYS to everyone in Stonehaven West!!!!

Date: Wed., 17 Dec. 1997

Hi everybody I found my kitten so don't bother looking anymore. But Thanks Anyway.

Date: Tues., 23 Dec. 1997

For those of you out there who have blue boxes filled and ready for pickup tomorrow, don't bother. The pickup was today (Tuesday). Garbage pickup which is normally scheduled for this coming Friday will be delayed until Saturday January 27. After this week the normal pickup schedule will fall back into place.

Date: Tues., 13 Jan. 1998

Hi Neighbours:
I am looking for a good chiropractor and / or massage therapist in the Newmarket area, can you recommend someone to me?

Date: Tues., 13 Jan. 1998

Hi — we have been going to Wellspring Common for massage therapy on Davis Drive — they have two excellent staff members — very effective. My wife and I have been going for months now to them. A good Chiropractor is at Reugg Chiropractor Clinic on Main Street — she is very effective as well.

Date: Sun., 25 Jan. 1998

Hi, I have just started a Sunday Sun route. Most of the people in this community have not been getting this paper. If you would like to subscribe to the paper please contact me.

P.S. The paper costs $1.50 each Sunday. You can pay direct to the Sun or let the carrier collect it from you.

Date: Mon., 26 Jan. 1998

Is there anyone looking for steady full time job! Ontario Outdoor Maintenance is looking for a driver who knows how to operate a snow plow, drive a pick-up truck with a trailer attached to it, and also operate industrial lawn mowers for the summer time. Pay is very good. If any one is interested please call the numbers below thank you. Ask for Tony (Owner).

Date: Sun., 31 May 1998

For anyone not aware, there were a number of car break-ins on Saturday night along Hilton Blvd. and perhaps along Best Circle. I lost a cellular phone but did contact the phone company to ensure that it had been disabled. If you have not checked your cars lately it might be a good idea to see if you also had a late night visitor.

Does anyone out there have information on the security company that has been patrolling the neighborhood for the past few weeks? There was someone walking the streets last night who claimed to be on patrol but he did not have the usual canine associate with him. I'm wondering if he was really legitimate.

Date: Tues., 21 July 1998

My name is Z and I am currently a stay at home mom with two little ones
— a daughter (19 months) and son (5 months). I'm wondering if there
are other stay at home moms out there who would like to arrange a get-
together regularly. Looking forward to meeting you.

Date: Thurs., 28 May 1998

This is such a great community. I have got a lot of positive feedback
about a street party. I called the town, and was told that we have to write
a letter to the Director of Corporate Services, stating where, when, why,
how. It takes about 2 weeks for them to approve it. The Town will then
provide barricades to block off the street. We cannot have tables or
barbecues on the street, to provide access for emergency vehicles.

Once again, I am so glad that my family chose this neighborhood to live.
It is so friendly, and the people are so helpful. I can't wait to meet
everyone, and make some lifetime friends.

CHAPTER 11

What Did They Do On-Line?

Video Telephones

We were keen to find out how our videophone application — Vid•IO — was used by the residents. Vid•IO uses a portion of the computer screen for images of both the caller and the receiver, with smooth motion and good synchronization between audio and video. A previous trial run by CulTech had connected one hundred students in residence at Calumet College, York University, with video telephones. It had determined that audio sync is the most critical factor for user comfort, followed closely by a high enough frame rate that the motion isn't "jaggy."

Vid•IO was an instant hit, but after a few months adult use declined significantly. This so-called honeymoon effect is common when a new technology is introduced for the first time. Usually, the waning interest is a result of the novelty wearing off, but in our case there was a different explanation. It appears that our videophone turn-off factor was related to Metcalf's law for networks — the value of a network varies as the square of the number of people connected. Translated into everyday language, this means that a network like our Vid•IO system will not be very valuable to users until there is a critical mass of other users on-line.

I've read stories about the early days of telephone use, before the technology was ubiquitous, when people would write letters to each other, setting dates and times for telephone conversations from public pay phones. In the case of our Vid•IO trial, there were only about one hundred homes connected, and the residents told us that not enough of their friends, relatives, or business associates were connected by Vid•IO to make it valuable for them. The outcome would have been very different, they told us, if Grandma, who doesn't live in Stonehaven West, could have seen little Johnny on his birthday. It is reasonable to expect that videophones will not become popular until high-speed connectivity becomes fairly widespread.

Interestingly, the children in the trial had a very different reaction to Vid•IO. They measured its value not by the number of relatives or co-workers on-line but by its ability to connect them with friends, current or new. Most of their friends lived in the neighbourhood and went to the same school. They would scroll through the Vid•IO user list and click on each home until they reached another kid who answered the videophone. Then they would talk to their friend or make a new one, someone who likely went to their school. So although their parents' usage declined, kids continued to be heavy users of the video telephones.

CD-ROMs without CDs

We developed a technology that allowed us to transfer commercial CD-ROMs to our servers' hard disks and make them available over the network. This enabled us to distribute a large amount of high-quality, media-rich content without spending tens of millions of dollars to create it from scratch.

There were a couple of big advantages in this for the users. First, they did not have to have a CD-ROM player. Second, they didn't have to buy the physical CD-ROMs. We posted a good variety of titles from several distributors in categories such as education (for kids and adults), leisure (including games), art, information, and health. On average, each household accessed one to two CD-ROMs per week. The level of use remained steady throughout the trial.

During the six-month period that began in March 1998, participants accessed CD-ROM content 2,219 times. The most popular CD-ROMs were children's titles. Although we had a good variety, these proved insufficient to satisfy the curiosity of our participants. So although use held steady, we had complaints that we were not "freshening the pot" frequently enough with new titles. It has become a truism of on-line use that new content needs to be added constantly, and that even if there is a large stock of titles, users want to know "what's new."

Program Your Own Radio Station

The biggest home run of the trial in terms of content use was Jukeboxx, our music-on-demand application. We had chosen to investigate whether users would take the time and effort to select the material they wished to hear and arrange it in the order they preferred. This music application differed significantly from commercial radio, and also from the downloading of music files that the record companies are promoting on the Internet. In our case, no copies were made on the local computer. Our service was more like listening to custom radio stations that you programmed yourself.

Users made lists of the music they wished to hear while doing housework or homework, entertaining friends, or taking part in any other activity they wanted. Their lists were stored on the network servers, and thus they could go a friend's house and access their lists there for an experience that was both personal and shared.

The music content became available on August 1, 1997. In the first six months, more than 8,000 selections were made by the participants in the 87 households. The average list contained eight selections (about half an hour of music), although this average is skewed by many log-ins that contained just a single selection.

There were many surprises in the research data. We had assumed that the largest user group would be teens, but they turned out to be less frequent users than other age groups. Eighty-one percent of selections were made by adults, and a large number of plays were by pre-teens.

In hindsight, the results don't seem so strange. Teens are very well served by radio stations and record stores in malls. They are at an age when peer pressure pushes them towards a hit-oriented menu shared by their friends, some of whom work at the local record stores. The kids working at the record stores speak their lingo and help provide a comfortable hang-out for this age group.

On the other hand, younger children and adults have largely been disenfranchised by the current commercial system for distributing music. The adults generally migrate towards jazz, classical, and easy-listening music, categories that are not carried in volume at the local malls. To make matters worse, the experience of asking a teenage salesperson about a children's record or a classical title is usually unsatisfactory for the potential customer. In our top-ten list, we found jazz titles, classical titles, and artists like the Spice Girls who appeal to younger kids.

The rule of thumb in the music industry is that the top ten titles represent the great majority of the activity on the radio and at retail stores. Our results were in direct contradiction to this. The top ten musical titles accounted for only 17 percent of the plays and the top fifty titles represented only 42 percent of the total.

Of the approximately 2,000 titles available, more than half were accessed at least once in the six-month trial period. Consequently, the record companies, including Sony, Warner, EMI, BMG, Attic, Anthem, and others, changed their view of on-line music. Previously, they had been concerned that on-line music use would cannibalize their retail sales. Since reviewing these results, however, they suspect that on-line delivery can build new incremental markets for titles that are not currently being sold in retail stores.

Within a year, Amazon.com had been launched and on-line record retailing had become a viable business. In general, the results we had uncovered were replicated by the experiences of on-line Internet retailers. On-line shoppers are not focusing on best-sellers, because they can get them anywhere. Instead, they are asking for back-list catalogues, hard-to-get titles that are not stocked at local outlets. Also, adult-oriented musical styles such as jazz and classical constitute a much greater share of sales on-line than they do in retail stores.

The trial results reinforce the view that many users will spend time and energy on interactivity if it produces something they value. When they were given the opportunity to program their own music channels, users took to it like ducks to water, generating play lists that were significantly different from those of commercial radio stations or the inventories of record stores.

Education

As a side project to the Intercom Ontario trial, CulTech Research Centre, in collaboration with York University and Bell Canada, designed interactive on-line courses that were delivered on campus at York, but were also available to residents participating in the trial. Any Intercom user, of any age, could access these university courses, which included An Introduction to Computers, Introduction to Multimedia and the Web, Personal Communications, and Telecommunications Policy.

The participants at home could learn from these on-line courses, but they did not have the benefit of tutorial help from the university faculty, nor did they receive credits for their efforts. On the other hand, they could have had both by enrolling at the university and paying the normal course fee. The educational project was meant to be an early investigation into lifelong learning, the process by which each of us will likely continue our education in many ways throughout

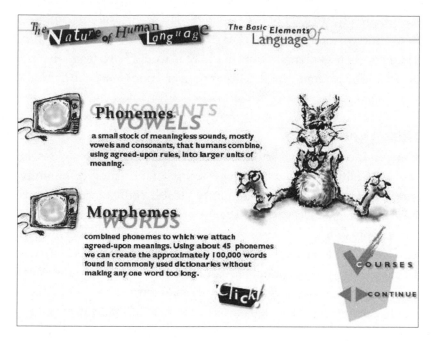

The *Nature* of Human *Language*   The Basic Elements Of Language

Phonemes
a small stock of meaningless sounds, mostly vowels and consonants, that humans combine, using agreed-upon rules, into larger units of meaning.

Morphemes
combined phonemes to which we attach agreed-upon meanings. Using about 45 phonemes we can create the approximately 100,000 words found in commonly used dictionaries without making any one word too long.

Click!

COURSES

CONTINUE

our lives, instead of restricting it to a set period of formal attendance at a school.

The figure above illustrates a page from one of the university courses. It was interesting to note that the university faculty members who gave these courses and supervised their construction came up with materials that were generally entertaining, often employing cartoon characters (as above) and game-like simulations that could capture and hold a student's attention. While these techniques are common in lower grades, they are generally absent in higher education, which has become textbook intensive. But our educators, freed from the monochromatic and static text on a page, leapt at the chance to provide more compelling material.

We also invested a great deal of time and energy in bringing the local public school on-line. We learned that the connection of a school to educational content has almost no value unless the staff and administration are behind the project, and unless they agree to participate and are trained to assist with the delivery of the learning applications.

By the time we were able to arrange for this training and institutional buy-in, there were only six months remaining in our trial.

Consequently, we did not have enough data to measure the efficacy and utility of the many innovative education applications we had planned, such as digital report cards that would have been directly accessible by parents, parent-teacher conversations mediated by video telephones, and so on.

Health Care

Counsel Inc., a trial consortium member, worked with us to deliver an on-line health service. This integrated several existing community services, and included a community health toolkit with links to health-related services within the community. The health package focused on wellness (illness and injury prevention). Residents filled in on-line questionnaires that included their health histories and vital statistics. These were optional for all concerned, of course, since they are of a very delicate, personal, and private nature.

We designed the health database so that no one individual's information could be accessed, although the aggregate statistics could be totalled. Those participating could then chart and compare their personal statistics with the averages in the neighbourhood and nationwide.

The second part of the application (Nurse On Call) allowed participants to access a health-care professional twenty-four hours a day. So a parent wakened by a child with a high fever at 3 a.m., say, could get a consultation before deciding whether to drive to a hospital.

In our trial, the health-care professional was accessible only by telephone because we did not have the resources to connect the local hospitals and health-care services to the broadband community net. If we had been able to, there could have been a mediated, face-to-face conversation using the videophones, and perhaps some diagnosis would have been possible using the visual tool. Certainly, this will become an important part of health services as habicons increasingly come on-line with high-speed connections.

Our Team

We were fortunate to have project managers who could command the respect of all the partners, manage the complicated technical work, and bring personal dedication to their jobs. The first of these was Bob

Campbell, who left Bell Canada to work with us. He brought his expertise and personal contacts, and never wavered in his belief that communities connected by fat pipes would define a new user-empowered economy. Tom Jurenka, a senior partner in the software company Disus, followed him. Disus, one of the consortium members, was a financial dwarf in comparison to our large entertainment, telecommunications, and computer industry partners, but the company contributed Jurenka's services for more than a year, justifying our belief that we should be open to organizations of all sizes.

I have heard many favourable comments about the quality of applications developed at CulTech and many questions about the size of our development team. The applications for video telephones, the user interface, the CD-ROM access, and Jukeboxx music-on-demand were all developed by a tiny team that worked extremely quickly. Damian De Shane-Gill, head graphic designer, and Sash Katsnelson, head programmer, came to CulTech after graduating from York University courses in design and computer science. Under my direction and that of two of my fellow faculty members, Jerry Durlak and Peter Roosen-Runge, they developed these robust and highly rated applications over a period of only a few years. Our development process was as different from a large corporate effort as you could imagine. We put our faith in a few talented young people, gave them periodic oversight, and let them run with the ball.

Internet Web Sites

In addition to having access to the novel applications that we designed from scratch, users could venture onto the public Internet, much as they could from a private network like AOL. In our trial, the use of proxy servers and other sophisticated technologies gave our residents extremely fast Internet access, about 400 times faster than that of a dial-up modem. This portion of our service was very similar to the high-speed Internet services now being offered throughout North America.

CHAPTER 12

And Then It Ended

B Y THE END OF 1998, MOST OF THE APPLICATIONS WE WISHED to test had been deployed and tested. The network worked. The intellectual property management system that tracked everyone's activities worked. We would have liked to keep the network in operation for a much longer period of time so we could test longer-term impacts in the community, but events conspired to bring our trial to an end.

The main problem was technology. The network we deployed was excellent but, as it turned out, too costly for the telcos or cablecos to make money with in 1999. They had both chosen to go instead with lower-bandwidth options such as cable-modems and DSL (digital subscriber lines), whose costs were more attractive than the hybrid fibre-coax system we used. And commercial Internet trials had demonstrated that most users found these mid-band networks satisfactory for surfing the Net.

Since telecommunications companies were not using the type of technology that we had, it became orphaned, and thus spare parts would eventually no longer be available. In addition, the cost of maintaining the network was extremely high because a separate technical team had to be assigned to service our needs, which had become unique in the telco world.

The result was that the consortium decided to dismantle the network at the end of 1998. Ours was not the first info-highway trial to have come and gone, but when we told the residents that we were turning their habicon off, they went ballistic. The listserv was buzzing for weeks with mostly nasty messages echoing the frustrations of participants that the network and its content were being shut down.

It was clear that although we had initially met with every resident in our university offices and explained that the trial was a non-commercial research endeavour (and thus that they did not pay for connectivity or appliances other than their computer and the video camera), they had come to rely on the services and content. What had started as a content test had become, for the participants, an entitlement they were not prepared to lose without a fight.

This resulting tumult was considered by many of the consortium members to be a very important research result of the trial, because along with the fuss about termination came offers from the residents to pay for the services if we would agree to keep the community network in operation. More than half of the participants offered to pay $50 per month in fees if we would leave the network on.

Eventually, the Stonehaven West residents brought the issue to the front page of their local newspaper. The shut-down had become a major local news event, which was in broad contrast to most of the other info-highway trials, where the participants hardly noticed when the shopping and movie services were withdrawn. In the end, most of them migrated to commercial cable-modem and DSL services from local suppliers. Unfortunately, the best we could do for them was to shift their community listserv to the Internet and let them take control of it. Happily, they took ownership very quickly, and it continues to this day.

PART THREE

Infrastructures

CHAPTER 13

The Last Spikes

A S GOVERNOR OF CALIFORNIA, LELAND STANFORD WAS USED
to posing with a shovel in his hands or cutting a ribbon when a
new ship or building was commissioned, but those tasks didn't require
physical effort or dexterity. That all changed when, as one of the
heads of the Central Pacific Railroad, he was required to drive the last
spike to complete the rail line that would connect a continent.

In May 1869, this ceremonial completion of national infrastructure drew a crowd of onlookers so large that an army detachment had
to be brought in to clear a path so the important speakers and guests
would be unruffled by the rabble. The event had been hyped by the
railways, the government, and the press as if it were an inauguration,
a moment of great civic importance.

The Civil War had provided the necessary end to the political log-
jam that had blocked the project. Until the war erupted, congressional
representatives had argued endlessly over which of three proposed rail
routes through the Rockies should be chosen. The decisions made
about which towns would be on the route would determine who would
have access to affordable goods and transportation and who would not,
which states would see population growth and which wouldn't, who
would be rich and who would be poor. These same issues are echoed
at the turn of the twenty-first century. The routes today are virtual,
but we still speak of the info-rich and the info-poor, and of the potential disenfranchisement of those without connections.

When the South seceded from the Union, the North was free to choose its preferred northern route to Sacramento. But the war also provided an important additional impetus to the project. With the United States unquestionably linked from north to south, the transcontinental railway became more relevant because it would link the country from east to west, completing the image of a nation connected from sea to shining sea. This nationalistic metaphor helped deliver the congressional votes necessary to finance the construction of the railway infrastructure.

Although the government provided financial support, the underlying imperative for the connectivity was economic. The gold rush of 1849, twenty years earlier, had provided that commercial impetus. The opportunities in the West, where the ground was literally paved with gold, provided an economic pull so powerful that travellers and supplies were sailing around the South American capes or making the 300-kilometre overland trek across mountains, deserts, and hostile Native territories just to get there. Stanford was not worried about filling his rail cars with money-making traffic. The passengers and freight were already there, waiting to make their trips with greater speed, safety, and reliability. Five days after the linking ceremony, passengers began filling cars on the Omaha-to-Sacramento run at fares ranging from $111 (first class) to $40 (with no amenities), significant chunks of cash in those days.

The Central Pacific's Jupiter locomotive steamed up to within a few feet of the end of the line, waiting like an immensely heavy and powerful beast, clouds of hot steam pouring out of its orifices, an icon for the age that brought connectivity and prosperity to the old and new worlds. It was a fitting image for the revolution that enabled rail travel. The gears, heavy machinery, and raw power were emblematic of industrialization. But even the best minds back then could not foresee the implications of the massive changes that were taking place — nor the changes in lifestyle or the dangers to the environment.

Like the coal-burning locomotive, the nineteenth-century factories of mass production spewed smoke that would later be found to poison the atmosphere and create a global warming that would melt glaciers and wreak havoc with farming and fishing. But in 1869, the most apparent change was in the mindset of ordinary people. Worried at first about losing their jobs, most people had finally accepted the notion that changes enabled by new technologies were both necessary and beneficial. There was an excitement surrounding the completion of the rail link that would be matched by the first landing on the moon one hundred years later.

A lone telegraph operator, Jackson Johnston, was tasked with communicating to the world at large the exact moment when the last spike was driven. He too was caught up in the merriment, tapping his foot in time to the band and trying to soak up the importance of the moment. He had just sent, in Morse code, a message that travelled instantly along the telegraph wires that were the companion infrastructure to the railway tracks. "All ready now," Johnston relayed to the world. "The spike will soon be driven. The signal will be three dots for the commencement of the blows."

The entire nation waited for these three dots to signal the start of local parades and ceremonies. But when Stanford's great moment came, he missed the ceremonial golden spike and came within a millimetre of crippling his left foot. Ever the politician, he quickly regained his composure and exclaimed, "Here, Tom, your turn." Thomas Durant was Stanford's counterpart from the East, the vice-president of the Union Pacific Railroad, and his company's endeavours were represented by Engine 119, which was facing the Jupiter locomotive.

The two beasts were separated by only about ten metres on that May day at Promontory Point, Utah. The engineers were waiting for that final blow to the spike so they could move towards each other and make the symbolic connection of their cowcatchers. Durant took the heavy hammer from Stanford and carefully aimed at the golden spike. He raised the sledge and then watched it descend, landing with a huge bang. The spike and silver hammer were both wired to a telegraph line so they would make an electrical connection and send a signal through the nation's network to proclaim the completion of the transcontinental railway.

Cameras clicked. The huge crowd erupted in hurrahs. Only those close to him noticed that Thomas Durant, too, had missed the spike.

But it didn't matter. The Union Pacific's chief engineer quickly stepped up and hammered the spike into place as the two opposing locomotives inched towards each other and touched.

Pandemonium broke out. Hats were tossed in the air, people danced, and the beginning of a new era of connected communities was born. The event set off the first simultaneous nationwide celebration: in San Francisco and New York, at the moment of contact, two cannons facing the Pacific and the Atlantic fired shots, symbolizing that the United States was also prepared to extend its newly united presence outward.

Canada's Last Spike

Neither Stanford nor Durant could have known that sixteen years later, under very different circumstances, another last spike would be driven to complete the Canadian transcontinental railway at Craigellachie, British Columbia. Why were the circumstances so different? Well, to begin with, Canada, although it was a much larger country than the United States, had a population of just over 3 million, hardly the financial base to support the extravagant $250,000 the U.S. government had spent on its "last spike" celebration. Also, the United States had many well-developed cities at the time, while Canada was still largely unexplored and uncharted. But perhaps the most significant difference lay in the reason each government decided to back its railway infrastructure in the first place.

The American push to connectivity was driven by economic imperatives, but in Canada the endeavour was driven by the need for national community. The American gold rush had established destinations such as Sacramento, where hordes of prospectors, opportunists, settlers, and investors flowed. The rail link was built to make it easier for East Coast business interests to reach those destinations. It was a classic case of business opportunities driving traffic. On the other hand, Port Moody (near Vancouver), the western terminus for the Canadian Pacific Railway, was not a particularly desirable destination for business. Instead, the Dominion of Canada, which had been created only two years before the U.S. transcontinental link was completed, needed connectivity for fundamental nation building.

The nationalism so prevalent in the United States was founded on its separation from England and nurtured by a hundred years of nationhood and the Civil War, events that had no parallel in Canada, whose history was just beginning. In Canada, the imperative for the transcontinental was political. When British Columbia was admitted to the Dominion of Canada on June 20, 1871, a condition of its entry was that a railway be built to connect the new province with the rail system of Eastern Canada. Fourteen years later, after the Canadian government had provided 25 million dollars, 25 million acres of land, and the existing railway lines from Port Arthur through Winnipeg to Emerson and from Port Moody to Savona, the Canadian Pacific was finally completed.

The "last spike" was struck at Eagle Pass in the Rocky Mountains on November 7, 1885. At the frugal Canadian ceremony, only a silver spike was to be used (gold was held to be too costly). But the silver spike was never hammered in — a common iron one was substituted at the last moment to keep the ceremonial spike untarnished.

Donald Smith, the director and largest shareholder of the Hudson's Bay Company, was the person designated to hammer the last spike. He inadvertently managed to mirror his U.S. counterpart when he too missed the mark with his blow, bending the spike. Finally, with the assistance of the road master, Frank Brothers, the bent spike was replaced with a fresh one and hammered home.

The Canadian event was low-key. Pierre Berton, in his book *The Last Spike*, describes the moment as follows: "Smith posed with the uplifted hammer. The assembly froze. The shutter clicked. Smith lowered the hammer onto the spike. The shutter clicked again. . . . Save for the blows of the hammer and the sound of a small mountain stream gushing down a few feet away, there was absolute silence." After the spike was set, William Cornelius Van Horne, the general manager of the Canadian Pacific Railway, made the following characteristically understated Canadian speech: "All I can say is that the work has been well done in every way. All aboard for the Pacific."

Van Horne had good reason to be subdued. In contrast to his southern counterparts, he had no significant traffic waiting to travel on his railway. Indeed, the lack of compelling Canadian destinations worried Van Horne back then, much as it worries the directors of today's digital routes. He understood that without desirable destinations, people would not fill his rail cars and there would be no profit for his venture.

His response to this problem was inspired. He raised millions of additional dollars to create the fabulous Canadian Pacific hotel chain and the tourist destinations of Banff, Lake Louise, and Victoria. By packaging the picturesque beauty of the land with kitschy Native guides, gourmet cooks, and luxurious accommodations, he created unique destinations that could be accessed only by rail. Van Horne recognized that there was no viable Canadian "business case" to be made for the railway infrastructure at the time it was built. It was all economic push, not economic pull.

Interestingly, the same thing has taken place more than a century later, with Internet companies rushing to provide compelling destinations for digital connectivity routes. The shortage of these destinations has left many infrastructure providers with poor business scenarios, which in turn has stalled the deployment of the so-called information superhighway.

By the time the transcontinental railways were finished in the United States and Canada, more than 60,000 kilometres of infrastructure had been laid at the cost of more than $1 billion. In both cases, the connectivity was expensive, highly risky, and generously subsidized by government. But without these national infrastructures, the United States would not have emerged as a superpower in the twentieth century and Canada would not have become one of the world's most prosperous nations.

CHAPTER 14

How Wide Is the Web?

ALTHOUGH RAIL CONSTRUCTION WAS AN EXPRESSION OF THE industrial age, historians have begun to compare its impacts with the impacts of information routes on communities today. Edward Rothstein, in his book *Looking at the Transcontinental Railroad as the Internet of 1869*, notes the significance of "the way that [the railways] altered the surrounding cultural universe with Internet swiftness."

The railways had an enormous impact on all aspects of late-nineteenth- and twentieth-century life. They weakened the established social structure and created new classes of haves and have-nots based on connectivity. They changed the locations, demographics, and populations of cities, and led to businesses that were more ambitious in scale than had previously been possible. This, in turn, led to the beginnings of the modern stock market. The immensely speculative nature of railway stocks, when coupled with their ability to return huge multiples of original investments, led to a period in which much of the new wealth was created by the capitalization of railway-related companies. Most of these companies would not have found favour with investors except for the fortunes that were being made daily from their stocks, whose values soared on tidbits of encouraging news or promotional hype. This period of wealth expansion and economic good times is very similar to what we are experiencing today with Internet-related stocks.

There were also countless start-up businesses whose livelihood was tied to the railways, from catalogue companies that relied on the timely delivery of their products to circuses that relied on the quick and cost-effective transport of animal caravans. Again, there is a parallel to the digital revolution, which has seen companies like Federal Express experience huge growth because Internet shoppers need to have their goods delivered quickly. In the late 1800s, as is still the case today, the short-term profitability of these new and fashionable companies was less important to investors than the fact that they were getting in on the ground floor of operations that would not have been possible without the new infrastructure. Then, as now, these early risk-takers were proven correct, as the huge numbers of overnight rail and Internet millionaires attest.

The speed of these changes was dizzying in the 1800s, as it is today. Trade multiplied, distances shrank, and ordinary people grew impatient with traditional transport. An observer in 1830 noted, "What was quick is now slow; what was distant is now near." Sounds like the seeds of the global village!

Of course, the cost of building the rail infrastructure was enormous, even greater than the cost of building a digital infrastructure today. Investors and governments paid more than $1 million (in today's currency) per kilometre of track for the transcontinental railway. By contrast, the cost of laying a kilometre of fibre-optic cable today is only about $10,000 — one-hundredth the earlier amount. The transcontinental railways could not have been built in the United States or Canada without government assistance, because the infrastructure was not able to produce a return on investment in a short enough period to satisfy investors. But public money and support were provided for rail connectivity because people believed that all citizens would eventually profit, that the quality of their lives would be improved, and that their sense of nationhood would receive a substantial boost.

One can also make these arguments for digital connectivity at the turn of the twenty-first century, although the political context has not been fertile ground for these seeds of reason to grow. We are just emerging from a quarter century of decreased government spending and intervention, a time when short-term corporate profits have overridden plans to create a better future for our children. The notion that governments should provide assistance for infrastructure has not been popular and may not be popular in the future — unless, of course, we see the emergence of lobbying groups powerful enough to override the prevailing mood and influence legislators.

One such group in the United States is the broadcast television lobby. This group, forced to concede that the analogue television system would have to be replaced with expensive new infrastructure, succeeded in influencing Congress to pass legislation giving broadcasters $1 trillion of digital bandwidth for free, provided they convert to a digital television infrastructure and deliver digital programming. As a result of this agreement, each broadcast undertaking receives a free digital channel on which it can deliver a combination of television, Internet, cellphone, messaging, and other digital services. In return, the broadcasters turn off their analogue channels, something they would have had to do in any event, although not so quickly.

High-Speed Always-On Networks

When it comes to other high-speed (i.e., video-capable) network alternatives, there have been no industry groups cohesive enough to push for government assistance. The reason for this can be traced to the genesis of the Internet, which was assembled with no administrative structure and hence has no industrial lobby clearly identified with it. Consequently, the penetration of high-speed connectivity and the enabling of habicons has been slower than expected. For the most part, this connectivity is being driven by the short-term money-making opportunities that are visible to the myopic telcos and cablecos. Now is the time for the needs of communities, the unemployed, the less well-to-do, the elderly, and the technically challenged to be taken into account by governments.

There is no need for us to create a society of info-rich and info-poor. We need not have sections of our population wither simply because the info-route bypasses their communities. A quick general move to high-speed connectivity would benefit all, because on-line connectivity conforms to Metcalf's law, which states that the utility of a network varies as the square of the number of connections. In plain words, this means that if you double the number of people connected to a network, that network becomes four times more valuable to each person on-line. Connecting everyone to a high-speed network, then, not only assists those who otherwise might not be able to participate in the digital revolution, but also brings much higher value to service providers, infrastructure companies, cyber-consumers, and other netizens.

The telephone networks provide a good model for this type of network. Your telephone has enormous value because you can call almost anyone, contact almost any organization. There is no need for a killer application because the killer application is *everything and everyone*. Telephone service is valued highly because of its ubiquity. The same is true of television, a service that was initially free but now costs hundreds of dollars annually in cable and specialty fees. In spite of television's ever-rising cost, very few people give it up. Like the telephone, the television is extremely valuable because everybody has one.

E-commerce businesses would certainly want everyone to be connected by broadband because statistics about on-line buying show that users who have high-speed access make purchases at double the rate of those who use dial-up modems. Although high-speed connectivity is touted for its ability to deliver faster access to web sites, research shows that two other functions — always-on service and the ability to support real-time audio and video — are of much greater importance. Telcos and cablecos offer high-speed access using different technologies (DSL versus cable-modems), but both feature always-on service. This means that users do not have to dial their service provider, log in, and wait for a connection before they can begin using the Net. High-speed users are connected continuously, so they can keep their e-mail, web browser, and other Internet connections active all the time. As a result, high-speed users find the on-line experience much more satisfying than their dial-up counterparts do.

The second important advantage of high-speed access is its ability to deliver better-quality audio and video. Instead of the jerky images and stuttering audio that are hallmarks of dial-up modems, high-speed connections allow you to use the Internet like a telephone, listen to radio stations with excellent fidelity, and receive reasonably smooth video images (although these are currently much smaller in size than television images).

As current service providers increase their bandwidth to and from your home, video telephones, video conferencing, and other forms of visually linked collaborative work and play will become increasingly available. William Bane and Stephen Bradley, in an October 1999 *Scientific American* article, equate today's low-speed modem connections with learning to ride a bicycle using training wheels — you can get hooked on the experience even before you get to travel at higher speeds. They state, "Even in its current nascent stage, [the Internet] has successfully engaged consumers, unleashed creative forces within enterprises, and connected previously disparate individuals into virtual communities."

The speed of adoption of the Internet has been unprecedented. It took thirty-six years from the time telephones were introduced for one-third of American households to acquire one. Thirty-eight years passed before that same percentage had radios, 13 for television, and 10 for cable television. The Internet has achieved that level of penetration within 5 years, and that has been without the more compelling high-speed, always-on, video-rich access.

CHAPTER 15

Access and Ubiquity

I REMEMBER WHEN IBM FIRST INTRODUCED THE PERSONAL COM-
puter in 1980. It was an exciting development because IBM was a
huge company whose name was synonymous with reliability and
technical excellence. Many analysts believed that with IBM mass marketing the product, public acceptance for home use was just around
the corner.

They were wrong. A few years earlier, I had purchased an Apple
home computer after I cashed a royalty cheque for one of my film
scores and then walked past a window display at a computer shop. I
bought the computer and one of each book, software program, and
plug-in card then available. Most other PC users at that time were
hobbyists, engineers, or electronic technicians who were interested in
playing with the bits and bytes. But my interests were music and ani-
mated graphics, which meant there were almost no application programs available for me.

Steve Wozniak had not yet invented the disk-drive card that was
to allow Apple computer users the great utility of floppy disks, so
all software programs had to be keyed in manually or loaded from
audio cassettes. You got your programs from hobbyist magazines,
which published the code line by line, or from pre-recorded cassette
tapes, which stored the digital computer bits as sing-song audio tracks
that sounded much like modem traffic does today.

It was clear to me at the time that ordinary people would not immediately flock to PCs. I was hooked, but of course I was considered eccentric by most of my friends. I even had a cool sign on the door of my living room, a holdover from the sixties and seventies that read: "Whoever has the most toys when he dies wins." I thought it was funny, given the increasing array of computer cards and piles of software manuals and floppy discs that adorned my home, but my friends thought it puerile and stupid. As I began to meet other guys (PCs were a mostly male pursuit back then) who had computers, I noticed that they also had cool signs like mine and indulged in humour that I found funny but that escaped most ordinary folks.

I had found my niche. These were my people. They all sensed that the language of bits and bytes, when coupled with the power of microchips, would cause a revolution that would affect all aspects of work and play. Our belief was not shaken one iota by the fact that at the time there were very few useful things one could do with a PC.

To get my computer to output musical sounds and graphics, I had to learn to program the inner guts of the machine with a user-unfriendly language known as machine code. I brought my computer into our bedroom because my wife was bedridden at that time, and it allowed me to keep busy while being available if she needed assistance. I spent about six months of twenty-hour workdays devoted entirely to programming, fiddling, going out to buy a new printer or other attachment, shunning family mealtimes, and avoiding social contact. I was a nerd before the word came into general use.

At the end of that period, however, the results of my handiwork were apparent: I had created three application programs. The first was a music program that allowed my Apple to sequence rudimentary quasi-musical sounds using an add-on synthesizer card. I used this in a television commercial soundtrack for Agree shampoo, and the jingle-production company I worked for won an award (although the sound was cheesy, it was also unique and catchy for the times). That allowed me to hold up my head for the first time and claim that all my work had a practical use.

The second application I wrote was an animation program. I created a simple means of entering drawings (pixel by pixel) into the computer, giving them names, and then making them move up and down or rotate. After endless hours, I was able to create a car that slowly moved across the monitor screen, complete with turning wheels. I thought this was a great accomplishment, but when my family and friends saw it, they immediately noted that it was inferior to even the most primitive cartoons, which in those days were created without the aid of computers.

My third application was one that balanced our bank statements at the end of each month. It took me more than a year to write the code, both because I had no formal computer training and because I had to teach myself a new computer language for just about every application I tackled. In addition, I had no idea how accounting systems worked. Nonetheless, the Hoffert chequebook-balancing program was a good solution for the needs of our small home-based business. I had acquired a floppy disk drive by then, and I proudly proclaimed that our financial data could now be stored in our safety deposit box in case of a catastrophe, such as a tornado hitting our house or our dog eating one of the disks (this happened once). My kids drearily reminded me that we could put paper records in our safety deposit box just as easily as floppy disks, but I loved my computer and could not imagine doing without one. Eventually, my family grudgingly admitted that the accounting program was useful, but they reminded me that they could do the job in half the time without a computer.

At first, most PCs languished unused in closets because the available software wasn't useful to non-business people. It was hard to justify using a PC spreadsheet for home finances unless you had a complex investment portfolio or ran a business from your home, in which case you were really using your computer for business, not personal, use. Moreover, most folks didn't write many letters, so the computer's word-processor application was overkill, particularly since you needed an expensive and agonizingly slow printer to get a paper copy that could be mailed. The dot-matrix printout was particularly unattractive, and the average typewriter was still a cheaper and more efficient means of writing letters.

Games were the most popular non-business application category in the early days. Before Nintendo introduced personal game consoles, PCs were the only way a kid (or an adult) could play an electronic interactive game at home. Although you couldn't possibly justify the cost of a PC if all you wanted to do was play arcade games like Pong or Pac-Man, those of us who bought them spent a great deal of time doing just that. Anyway, what else was there to do with the gizmos? Amazingly, two decades later, after the introduction of hundreds of new software applications and hundreds of thousands of technical improvements, gaming is still one of the most popular activities among those with home computers.

PCs didn't begin to become viable consumer appliances until they left the home and moved back into the office, the former domain of mainframes and mini-computers. The essential technical enabler, first in offices and then in homes, was connectivity. Some attribute the breakthrough in PC utility to Steve Jobs, in his first stint as CEO of Apple. Jobs mandated that every Macintosh PC would be manufactured with a built-in network connection. This meant that you could connect your PC to any others in your home (but who could afford more than one?), to a big computer at work, or to any one of the growing number of community bulletin boards, newsgroups, chat lines, and special-interest forums that were popping up in cyberspace. Of course, in the 1980s, there was not yet a clearly defined sense of cyberspace, that place where we communicate with non-human entities, sharing our visions, inspirations, interests, and idiocies in a time-shiftable domain.

Hello World!

The prophetic words "Hello World," the first line of programming many students learn, were crafted by Brian Kernigham and Denis Ritchie, the AT&T Bell Labs scientists who developed the C programming language (which was used to create the popular UNIX operating system). But "Hello World" was also a metaphoric wake-up call to the rest of us, a hint that the key to the widespread use of computers would be communication.

At first, the experience of connecting a PC to a network was not a particularly pleasant one for the uninitiated. Ordinary telephone lines were used to connect one computer with another (using modems), but these were sometimes noisy and always introduced errors. To overcome this, the text and computer programs we exchanged had to be encoded using complicated mathematical schemes that could recover the signals from the noise. Although we didn't have to understand how these schemes worked, we did have to select which ones would be used for any given communication session. And there were dozens of choices — seven or eight bits, handshaking on or off, and so on. If a sender's communication program was not set to the same specifications as a receiver's, no signals would get through.

When users finally did connect, the most popular activity was to type text to each other. A typical session looked something like this:

> *Can you read this?*
> >Can't read. Let me change some settings
> *How about now?* [Repeat the foregoing about five times.]
> >Read you loud and clear.
> *This is cool, eh?*
> >Yes. Do you have any new games?
> *I'm sending one now. It should take about an hour and a half.*
> >Cool.

These conversations were the precursors to e-mail. Indeed, having a mediated conversation with someone faraway continues to be the most popular activity for people with home computers. In 1992, the World Wide Web was invented, which brought the organizing concept of pages to the Internet, added the ability to link words and images to other pages, and removed the necessity for typed commands. Now you could point and click your way to . . . whatever. The floodgates opened, and connectivity began to drive computer sales.

People began to buy computers not so much for their productivity software, but because they could connect with sources of information and other people. Manufacturers began building in modems because their inclusion was driving sales. And finally, there was a killer app for home computers: the Internet browser. As stand-alone appliances, home computers had not been able to penetrate the consciousness of ordinary people, but when they became a means of connecting with *other* people the idea took hold.

Soon, more than half of North Americans owned a computer. By 1999, a survey reported by CyberAtlas of Internet users in eighteen countries found that levels of penetration had become higher at home than at work. By the turn of the century, home computers had achieved a significant enough market share to be considered consumer appliances. Like refrigerators and stoves, they are now accepted by some mortgage companies as part of the purchase price of a home, provided they are located in a home-office environment.

It is ironic that, just as PCs are finally being accepted as a standard consumer device, most experts believe their days are numbered. The microchips at the heart of PCs are becoming so powerful and inexpensive that they are being embedded into other simpler appliances, which will eventually provide many of the functions performed by PCs today. Scientists at Bell Labs, where the transistor and the laser (among other items) were invented, predict that by 2025 we will all be wired into a "global communications skin." This communications network will use devices as small as lapel pins to sense everything from weather patterns to how much milk is in your refrigerator.

Arun Netravali, the president of Bell Labs, says, "We are already building the first layer of a mega-network that will cover the entire planet like a skin. . . . Thermostats, pressure gauges, pollution detectors, cameras, microphones — all monitoring cities, roadways, and the environment. They will transmit data into the network, just as our skin transmits a constant stream of sensory data to our brains."

This idea of embedding computing power in devices that communicate with each other is at the heart of much of the ongoing research and development at major companies like Bell Labs, IBM, and Xerox. And the concept of connected devices works hand in hand with our concept of connected communities, which provide part of the infrastructure needed for these devices to function. To understand the roles of computers, telephones, televisions, and other appliances in habicons, it is helpful to examine digital connectivity at the national, local, and personal levels.

CHAPTER 16

Wide Area Networks

THE MICROCHIP IS THE FOUNDATION OF NEW DIGITAL TECH-
nologies, an enabling tool as revolutionary as the wheel or fire.
The digital language of zeros and ones is a common basis on which all
tools can interoperate. This is what makes it possible for you to download your calendar and phone book from your computer to your digital watch just by aiming it at the screen. It also enables the CD player
in your computer to understand computer programs, educational
courses, photographic archives, music, games, and Hollywood movies.

But today's digital technology deals with more than the electronic
circuits in those consumer appliances. It also deals with light. And the
most pervasive use of optical technology is in our wide area networks
(WANs). These are the successors to the original copper-wire long-
distance telephone lines. Their capacity and reliability have driven up
communications traffic exponentially. Though they once carried only
telephone traffic, they now carry data transfers, faxes, and television
signals (which must be translated to digital formats for carriage and
then back to their analogue form for display on TV sets).

The bandwidth of these WANs is enormous and increasing daily.
The North American continent is criss-crossed with multiple fibre-
optic strands that carry the light-modulated signals to and from all
centres of industry and population. For mission-critical applications
such as bank-to-bank transactions, the system has enough redun-
dancy in it that a signal disruption in one fibre-optic line will cause

information automatically to be switched to another line over a different geographic route.

In "The Effect of Multimedia Telecommunications on the Global Environment," a 1993 paper I co-authored with Dr. Martin Hoffert and Eric Hoffert, we noted that a single hair-like strand of fibre-optic cable has the innate capacity to carry about 6 billion pages of text per second or more than one million high-resolution television channels. And what is this miracle cable made of? Glass . . . which is cheap and abundant. But the capacity of fibre-optic cables has not yet been matched by the electronics that connect to them, which transform electronic currents and voltages to modulations of a laser light beam. Every six months or so, the interfacing electronics improve significantly and the capacity of the networks increases. And this takes place without any additional fibre being laid.

The technology is so reliable and cost-effective that every industry uses it as the "backbone" of distribution. Cablecos use it for television signals. Telcos use it for telephony. And just about every organization that owns a long-distance right-of-way, such as a railway or an electric utility, has thousands of miles of fibre strung along its properties.

Because there are so many types of applications and so much content sent over these fibres, standards and protocols of transmission have been developed that allow each type of signal to coexist with others simultaneously. The WAN standards, however, have been adopted from the telephone industry while the standards used in institutions, businesses, and homes have come from the computer industry.

Standards

The U.S. standard railway gauge (the distance between the rails) is 4 feet 8.5 inches. Why is this apparently odd gauge the standard? Because it's the same width as the distance between the wheels of Roman chariots. The story behind the adoption of this unusual standard provides a lesson for those involved with digital infrastructure — that is, the adoption of a standard frequently has more to do with interoperability than logic.

The Roman Empire was built on imperial standards that allowed it to administer its huge range of lands and cultures with military precision. There were standards for waterworks, standards for money, and standards for roads. All roads needed to be the same width so that the Roman chariots could negotiate them. When the Roman Empire eventually extended into what is Britain today, the first long-distance roads were sized for imperial Roman legions and their chariots.

Over the years, wagons with newer technology came into vogue, but they retained the wheel spacing of the Roman chariots because to do otherwise would cause breakdowns on the existing roads, whose ruts were spaced according to the old vehicles. When steam-driven trams came into use, their builders used the same jigs and tools they had used for building wagons, and so the spacing remained the same.

Roads and wagons in North America, freed as they were from Roman history, initially developed in a variety of gauges, as did the first American railways, which mimicked the widths of local wagons. Europe led the way in the industrial production of trains, however, and many parts were exported from that continent to North America, so when problems arose with connecting American railways of different gauges, the European standard prevailed. As a result, North American railways use the 4 foot 8.5 inch standard that was used in Rome two thousand years ago.

The issue of standards becomes important whenever a new technology is expected to achieve wide distribution among the population. Colour television is another example of a technology standard that was adopted even though it was known to be inferior to other proposed schemes. The successful standard, however, was compatible with existing black-and-white TV sets, on which viewers could watch the new colour programs, albeit in black and white. Ultimately, economies of scale and the desire for interoperability drove the decision to go with the system we still use today. This same line of thinking is influencing modern-day decisions about standards for distributing information, communications, and entertainment on WANs.

Quality of Service

The WAN telephony standards have been optimized for what is known as quality of service (QOS). This has been the highest priority for telcos because the worst complaints from customers occur when a conversation is disrupted by poor-quality reception or outright disconnection.

There is no free lunch, and the need for QOS architectures that are relatively free of disruptions makes telephone networks much more expensive to design, build, and maintain than computer networks like the Internet. The Internet has not been primarily concerned with real-time distribution of audio and video, and so the standards that it uses require equipment and maintenance that is much less costly. After all, if a few bits in your e-mail message are garbled, your computer can send a message to the originating web site asking that those bits be re-sent. When they arrive, they are reassembled with the good ones and you are none the wiser when your message shows up on your screen correctly (a fraction of a second later).

But the lack of QOS on the Internet has been an obstacle to using it for general telephone and video service — until recently. There is a raging debate between the QOS folks (known in the vernacular as Bellheads) and the Internet folks (known as Netheads). The Netheads believe that the simpler and less costly equipment that is used for computer networks in businesses and increasingly in homes can also be used throughout the WAN with enormous savings in telecommunications costs. The Bellheads have been fighting this notion, primarily because they have trillions invested in telephone networks that will become worthless if the newer architecture is adopted.

The most widespread computer protocol is called Ethernet, and it comes as a built-in on most home computers. It has been used in universities, office buildings, and governments for dozens of years. The Netheads argue that although Ethernet cannot deliver the same quality of service as the WAN protocols (such as ATM and SONET), we can obtain the same results by dramatically increasing the bandwidth of the network. In simple terms, this means that having a much wider pipe makes it less likely that information packets will collide with each other and disrupt the flow.

The other implication of this approach is that Internet technology, which is based on inexpensive dumb networks, could be used for all types of communications. This means that computer equipment could be used end to end, and that the same inexpensive equipment and protocols that work on a local area network (LAN) could also be used on the WAN.

Remember the examples of standard railway gauges and colour television standards? The overriding factor that led to the adoption of the successful standard was its ability to interoperate. The pressure is therefore mounting to adopt digital standards that will make it easy and cheap for *anyone to connect his or her personal or community network to the WANs that girdle the globe.*

Unlike telephone networks, which constantly monitor transmission paths and intervene when a signal is disrupted, the Internet uses equipment that is oblivious to how and if a data packet arrives at its destination. The responsibility for fixing errors lies with the user's appliance, not with the network, and that's where the savings occur. The difference in the two technologies can be traced back to how scarce and expensive microchips were when our telephone networks were designed; today they are abundant, inexpensive, and built into most appliances.

Since both types of service can use the same fibre, it is expected that the next decades will see a great simplification and unification of WAN technology so that it can interoperate with consumer-grade products. Since this will lead to the use of many similar devices, the economies of scale will further drive down the price of connectivity and enable high-speed access for every home and office.

On September 15, 1999, the ResearchTV consortium and Sony Electronics Inc. reached a convergence milestone when they successfully sent HDTV (high-definition digital television) signals over the Internet, demonstrating the future of television. Soon the medium will be not only digital but also fully interoperable with the Internet, making today's separate television and telephone networks redundant.

This convergence of infrastructures is important for the future of habicon life, because although the first manifestations of community connectivity will require separate appliances for television, Web access, and telephony, subsequent appliances will be plug and play. A single integrated home environment will allow them to talk to each other and work together seamlessly.

Wireless Connections

Even though the majority of WAN transmissions will travel on fibre-optic cables, there are locations where wireless transmissions will still be more desirable. Some of these will be in communities that are isolated from other population centres, communities whose geographic locations present difficulties for laying cables, and Third World countries that have poor traditional infrastructures (roads) on which to lay cables. Like telecommunication and television signals today, some of these wireless signals will travel via satellites and others via ground-based wireless technologies. Both of these technologies are limited to the narrow band of frequencies known as microwaves, because only these frequencies can penetrate clouds for uninterrupted reception in all weather conditions.

LANs, however, will likely see more innovative use of wireless networks, and this brings the discussion back to habicons, because without question, community networks will be very important new links in the local telecommunications loop.

CHAPTER 17

Community Networks

ONE OF THE MAJOR CONCERNS PEOPLE HAVE ABOUT THE Internet is its lack of security. They fear that correspondence, transactions, and other activities will not be kept private. In the corporate and government worlds, these concerns are addressed by building private internal networks that use Internet protocols and give users access to many Internet activities. These, as we have seen, are called intranets.

Private intranets are first cousins to the public Internet, but they have the advantage of central administration and regulation, precisely the characteristics that are anathema to classic Internet users. The key to intranet security is a bridging device that has one side connected to the private network and the other to the Internet. This is known as a firewall. The intranet administrators can use it to prevent unwanted outside activity from intruding into their network, and also to control the types of access their users can have to the Internet. For example, an intranet e-mail system may be configured so that all employees have access to each other but not to ordinary Internet users. Conversely, junk e-mail (spam) and outsiders who would breach the privacy of internal documents can be excluded. The administrators also have the option of setting up a separate e-mail application that allows full access to and by outsiders.

Intranets, when confined to a single building or a group of buildings, are known as campus networks. When an organization needs to connect employees at several different campus locations, they set up a network known as an extranet. But there are also many private intranets that users do not differentiate from the global Internet, including America Online, CompuServe, and the cable-modem and DSL services offered by cablecos and telcos.

All of these share the same attributes. One of these is that users cannot be anonymous, as they can be on the Internet. Intranets have administrators, administrative controls, and, in the case of commercial intranets, signed agreements with users outlining the terms and conditions of network use. Those users who don't abide by the regulations can be found and disciplined. One might say that instead of the Internet's characteristic lawless Wild West atmosphere, intranets offer an environment in which law and order prevail.

It will become increasingly appealing for communities to operate their own private networks, and this may become a hallmark of habicons. For residents to feel comfortable engaging in the types of on-line conversations that we saw in the Intercom Ontario trial, they must know that these are confidential and closed to outsiders.

In order to build and operate high-speed community networks, communities will have to be able to easily acquire the fibre-optic transmission rights in their local area. As it turns out, this will be much easier than the entrenched suppliers would have us believe. Little by little, schools, companies, governments, and other organizations have been coming together to bypass the traditional bandwidth-supplying telcos and cablecos and "light" their own fibre networks. Lighting dark fibre is a process that has been kept out of the popular literature, not because it is too complicated but because the large industrial interests do not wish to draw attention to the simple building blocks of digital networks. After all, the more esoteric and hidden the inner workings of these systems remain, the less likely users will be to figure out the underlying economics.

Signals are sent along fibre-optic cables by shining a light (a very stable laser beam) through the glass fibre strands. The intensity of the light is modified (modulated) according to the type of input signals, which may be voice (sound), video, or data. At the other end of the fibre, a light detector senses the modifications in the basic laser light and decodes (demodulates) them back into the original signals.

Dark fibre is the infrastructure of cable bundles composed of these hair-sized fibre-optic strands. On its own, dark fibre cannot carry communications signals. But it becomes a conduit of communication when it is "lit" — that is, when equipment is attached to the fibre ends that send and receive modulated light. The dark fibre has a very low maintenance cost and a long life. Like computer electronics, its cost decreases over time as its capacity increases.

Controlling your own dark fibre allows you to match your capacity needs with your financial resources. Think of it as putting hi-fi speaker wires in the walls of your home. You can buy better amplifiers and speakers over time, according to your needs and your budget.

Building Your Own Network

Companies like National Fiber Network began laying municipal dark fibre in the early 1990s, with the objective of delivering digital signals to the doorstep of each home and workplace — the so-called last mile. In telephone parlance, this is known as the local loop (to differentiate it from long-distance WAN services).

National's business plan ran contrary to the status quo as espoused by the entrenched telcos and cablecos. Instead of using their copper and coaxial cable infrastructures to deliver digital network services, National ran massive quantities of fibre directly to the basements of end-users. They then began to sell the rights to these dark fibres by the mile on long-term contracts. National allowed its customers to decide how to light the fibre and what to carry on it.

National was bought by Metromedia Fiber Network in 1997, a move that made Stephen Garofalo, its founder, one of the wealthiest people in the United States. In a David Isenberg article in the December 1999 issue of *America's Network*, Garofalo explained his philosophy this way: "Selling dark fibre is like selling customers a fifty-story building for the price of the first floor. . . . If you need more room, you add more lights and switches and move upstairs." Garofalo started Metromedia after reading an article by George Gilder, a technopundit who sees the future of telecommunications infrastructure as dark fibre, dumb bandwidth, all-optical networks, and almost free communications for everyone. Gilder has long been predicting that bandwidth will soon be plentiful and low cost.

The economics of fibre optics hinge on the fact that, as I noted earlier, glass, the material used, is not costly or scarce. Almost all of the costs involved in laying fibre, in fact, are in acquiring rights-of-way and pulling the fibre between poles or in underground trenches. Indeed, the costs hardly change whether a company pulls two fibres or a dozen cables with hundreds of fibres in each cable.

When Metromedia pulls new fibre, it installs many more than current (and even projected) needs would dictate; it even installs empty conduits so it can pull additional fibre in the future. Once this infrastructure is in place, the cost of maintaining each fibre is close to zero. Metromedia's ultimate objective is nothing less than eliminating the telecommunications tariff system so that the newly abundant and regulation-free marketplace can determine the price of communications.

For now, about three-quarters of Metromedia's business comes from traditional telecom carriers. Most of its other business comes from data-intensive companies in the finance, medical, manufacturing, and public sectors. Although the company charges a low rate for leasing its fibres (compared with what telcos or cablecos charge), it does very well, thank you. In 1999, it booked more than $2 billion in leases.

All this proves that the expression "Build it and they will come" works admirably in this situation. Even when they install more bandwidth than they believe they need, business customers soon find that they require more capacity. This is because the availability of such high bandwidth greatly increases the use of the network, as does the very low cost of adding capacity. Users dramatically change the way they work, sending files over the network that they used to keep on their hard drives and making much more use of audio and video, traditional bandwidth hogs.

The economic model for increasing the capacity of fibre is fundamentally different from that of its copper-based predecessors. If you're using copper wires and need ten times the bandwidth, you'll have to use ten times as many wires at roughly ten times the cost. But you can increase the capacity of a single fibre by the same factor of ten simply by lighting it up with higher-bandwidth electronics (without using additional fibres). Consequently, the more bandwidth you use, the cheaper it gets.

Metromedia is only one of a growing number of players that are deploying their own dark-fibre plants. Other companies, such as Internet Fiber Inc., develop and install "last mile" fibre networks for new neighbourhoods and also place Ethernet HAN wiring in each home. The neighbourhood fibre and household Ethernet then become the property of the homeowners and are included in the purchase price. The neighbourhood association purchases Internet service from Internet Fiber or another supplier.

Many cities and states are already greasing the wheels for community networks by laying or leasing fibre and making it available to taxpayers at very low cost, thus bypassing the traditional carriers. Deborah Hurley and James Keller, in their book *The First 100 Feet*, note, "Local governments have a keen interest in the expected competition among telecommunication companies because the bulk of the technical infrastructure . . . is situated within the domain of municipalities. It is the city streets and poles that provide the real estate where telecommunication companies place their wires and hardware. . . . Furthermore for many cities, promotion of advanced telecommunications infrastructure is part of a broad strategic investment, which is meant to revitalize or sustain urban environments and to offer advanced services that may not be offered by incumbent telecommunications carriers."

In Virginia, the government provides universities, state agencies, and public schools with fast and cheap access through Net.Work.Virginia, which gets special rates from Bell Atlantic and Sprint because of its massive customer base. Cities such as Austin, Texas, San Diego, Seattle, Anaheim, Santa Clara, San Jose, and Palo Alto are also leading the charge, providing other municipalities with examples of how they can attract and keep businesses in the new economy.

Condominium Dark Fibre

There have been two predominant business models used in deploying fibre. The first is associated with traditional carriers, which value fibres according to their derived services, such as telephony, cable TV, or data carriage. A large portion of their costs are in the areas of marketing, advertising, promotion, sales, customer service, and government lobbying. They price their products in relation to the value delivered to their customers — and according to what the market will bear.

A second business model is embraced by dark-fibre entrepreneurs like Metromedia, companies that license long-term access to dark fibres and provide low-cost annual maintenance. Their fibre capacities are overbuilt and not yet well utilized, however, so their customers must bear the cost of idle facilities.

A third model is emerging that may well be a good fit for habicons, particularly if there are no vendors of dark fibre in the neighbourhood. This model is known as consortium-managed dark fibre. Local businesses, governments, and/or resident associations — known as the condominium — get together and pool resources to construct a fibre infrastructure that suits their needs. They then own and operate it, at a fraction of the cost of the other models. Cities such as Stockholm have been using this model, and they are treating fibre as a municipal utility. As a result, Stockholm has the lowest ISP rate on the European continent and has become the centre for broadband service innovations there.

In December 1999, CANARIE, a Canadian consortium of government, private-sector, and university telecom providers and users of high bandwidth, asked for bids for an Ottawa-area dark-fibre consortium, a managed infrastructure that is to use standard desktop computer architectures and extend them over a wide area. Each member of the consortium will pay for its portion of the construction costs and will be responsible for lighting up its own fibre strands. The result will be the deployment of low-cost broadband optical networks to homes, schools, and businesses.

This pilot project could serve as a model for other communities across Canada, and it could well permit Canadian enterprises to take the lead in developing services and applications in an environment where the cost of bandwidth is very low. In fact, Bill St. Arnaud, senior director of network projects at CANARIE, suggests that telecom infrastructure of the future will have hundreds of these customer-owned condominium dark-fibre networks interconnected with customer-owned wavelengths on longer-haul systems.

Customer-owned wavelengths are newer technologies that allow for different coloured lasers to light the same fibre strand, with each light frequency (colour) carrying different information. By renting specific light frequencies on a carrier's WAN infrastructure, consortiums that operate their own networks can communicate over long distances with privacy and security.

St. Arnaud suggests that eventually there may be a variety of separate optical networks under the control and management of individual customers. These could include a national optical network for K-12 schools, one for government services, several for large financial institutions, and so on.

The Réseau Interordinateurs Scientifique Québécois (RISQ) has been deploying condominium dark fibre at very low cost to Quebec schools and universities. The organization has demonstrated that a university can deploy a long-haul (in excess of a thousand kilometres) dark-fibre network for a much lower cost than a managed service from a carrier. This suggests that rural schools and libraries in remote areas may get high-speed connectivity for less than their sibling organizations in cities.

The numbers are difficult to ignore. In the Ottawa consortium, the twenty-two institutions — which include hospitals, government departments, research institutions, and universities — will each receive at least six dedicated fibres for a one-time cost of about $30,000 (plus about $300 annual maintenance). If this cost is amortized over twenty years, say, this means that each institution will have incredibly high bandwidth (almost unlimited) for less than $2,000 a year. That's the kind of economics and capacity that will help make high-speed communications a reality.

Perhaps the most interesting aspect of condominium networks is that they are a potential solution to the problem posed in the first section of this book: how do we counter the discomfort we feel in giving up control of our utilities and infrastructures to large corporations and governments? Here is an opportunity for local neighbourhoods to repatriate an increasingly important aspect of their lives.

CHAPTER 18

Home Area Networks

WE MOVE OUR ATTENTION FROM THE WAN AND THE LAN TO the home area network, the HAN. Most of us already have a few simple HANs in our homes. One example is our telephone network, which consists of twisted pairs of wires that run along the baseboards or in the walls. These wires terminate with standard telephone jacks that allow you to plug in several telephones, answering machines, and the like in different rooms of your home. A second network uses coaxial cables and cable connectors to provide the same sort of plug-in connectivity functions for televisions, VCRs, and so on.

The new HANs will be much more sophisticated and, most important, will integrate different types of appliances that today require separate networks. In addition to telephones and televisions, the new HANs will support computers and their related peripherals (such as printers, copiers, scanners, and fax machines), and will include networked storage for documents, photos, home movies, and CDs. HANs will even connect other home appliances, including refrigerators, stoves, toasters, and ovens, as well as the electric lights and the heating and cooling systems (these will be tied into your home security system). The balance of your entertainment appliances, including your stereo and DVD player, will be integrated as well.

To manage the diverse resources, you will have a computer that will sit in your utility closet and act as a combination file server and home management centre. It will not be overly costly by today's standards. In fact, we would all have these in our homes today if we had the wiring infrastructure and conversion hardware needed to make these diverse systems work with each other.

All of the devices enumerated above (and more) are already available with digital controls today, though not in every make and model. The problem has been one of standards and cost. Each industry has developed its own set of protocols and standards, and unfortunately, these have not worked with each other, so it has been impossible to have either integration or economies of scale.

But that is all changing. People want to be able to access their stereo in all the rooms of their home. Until recently they have been hindered by the cost of the wiring and installation, which alone has been several thousand dollars, and by the fact that such a system cannot be used to connect televisions, computers, or telephones. The same has been true for home security devices, which generally do not connect to your computer system, though they are digital. Even intercoms, which provide great utility in a home, are usually wireless (to save money on installation) and do not connect to your telephones, which contain most of the parts intercoms need to work (microphones, speakers, and amplifiers).

But the type of home automation that has been touted for more than twenty years now, the so-called smart home, will soon be a reality, with applications far beyond what the Jetsons cartoon envisaged in the 1960s. Until now, the best you could say about smart homes was that they were of slightly above average intelligence. The networks in tomorrow's habicons will turn them into geniuses.

The convergence of appliances, media, industries, and networks is the most important advancement to come out of the digital revolution. It enables interoperability, which means that a single home controller will be able to work everything. Of course, the downside is that if (when) it breaks down, you may have control of nothing.

The stumbling block of which standard to accept has been overcome by the wildfire-like growth of the Internet. It would have been hard to imagine in 1995, but today the Internet protocol (IP) and its associated universal resource locator (URL) addressing scheme have provided open, royalty-free standards that are being adopted across industrial boundaries. Together, these will make HANs a must-have utility for every home. In fact, new-home developers are routinely beginning to install HANs, whose cost is incorporated into home price and amortized over the term of the mortgage. Even renters will begin to demand HANs, as they do today with air conditioning. The Yankee Consulting Group predicts that 10 million homes in the United States will be equipped with home networks by 2003, a level of penetration that we saw first with computers and then with the Internet.

The greatest cost item for HANs has been the wiring, particularly in existing homes. In a new house or apartment building, it is not too expensive to string communications wires along with the electric cables inside the walls, but in existing homes it is very expensive to break holes in the walls, pull new cables, reseal the holes, and repaint or re-wallpaper. Consequently, the concept of HANs for everyone has stalled. But recent advances in home-wide wireless networks should make these available to all, at low cost.

In 1999, for example, Apple Computer introduced the first mass-market, inexpensive wireless home computer network. A user need only buy a base station for a few hundred dollars and a card for any devices that need to be on the network, such as computers or printers. Without any further connections, all the devices can immediately communicate with each other using radio waves, which travel through walls. Bingo, no more need for pulling cables. And no more need for *buying* cables. Future wireless products will make it as easy for you to communicate with appliances throughout your home as it is to use your television remote control today.

CHAPTER 19

Television

THE NOVEMBER 1999 ISSUE OF *CANADIAN BUSINESS* RAN THE headline "How the Internet Killed Television." It is noteworthy that the editor chose to use the past tense. Finally, here was a respected consumer publication acknowledging what everyone close to the television business has known for years: the model for commercial television, which uses advertising revenue as the engine for program creation and infrastructure funding, doesn't work any more.

The original implied contract between the viewer and North American broadcasters was based upon indirect taxation of all consumers. The price of the goods we purchase is inflated by the cost of advertising, but we accept the tariff because it brings us "free" television programming.

That contract broke down with the advent of cable television. Cablecos initially charged fees for connectivity — extending your antenna, so to speak, so you could receive a better signal. When they started also offering program content, some of it not available from broadcasters at any location, cable and wireless providers in effect changed their business models. They began charging a monthly fee for content as well as connectivity, even though the programs they aired still carried advertising. Today, average viewers pay about $500 a year for their cable programs, and those who don't watch the television services still have to pay the inflated price for products that advertise on TV.

Although most consumers don't currently associate the high cost of goods and services with their television content, I believe this will change. Advertising continues to permeate every aspect of twenty-first-century life, and now even the Internet, which is beginning to replace television, has succumbed to an advertising model.

Before 1993, no advertising or commercial services were permitted on the Net. But that meant Internet companies were saddled with the problem of raising huge amounts of capital to deliver infrastructure and content for which there was no solid business model. The main thing the Internet had going for it was that users really liked it. That fact was enough to tempt advertisers into jumping on board the speeding Web train, injecting the capital that was needed for new growth. When netizens allowed ads to come on-line, the future of both networked communications and television was changed forever.

Today, advertising has become the dominant model for financing Web content and web site production. On the Net, advertising no longer need be the "one size fits all" model that it is on television because the network's interactivity means each viewer can be treated differently. Some may wish to pay a monthly fee in lieu of receiving advertising, for example, while others may agree to watch advertising and participate in longer marketing sessions in exchange for a credit on their monthly content or connectivity bill.

The stock market now looks to advertising revenue and networked commerce as bellwethers of Internet dot-com success. Although early numbers were difficult to correlate, advertisers have now agreed that there is good value on-line. This has affected television broadcasters and content producers in three significant ways. First, the huge variety of content available on-line has encouraged the diversification of television channels, program content, and viewer demographics, moving that one mass market towards ever narrower markets, which is why we now have whole channels devoted to golf, cooking, and specific musical styles.

Because so many additional channels (satellite television services now offer up to 900) and thousands of additional programs are being produced each year, the average program budget has been declining. After all, advertisers don't have more money to spend just because more programs are being produced. Thus television's biggest advantage over the Internet — its high production values — has started to evaporate.

Second, as advertisers began to spend significant sums on-line, this money was cannibalized from television budgets, further diminishing the funding pot for that medium. The problem for commercial television is exacerbated because as more viewers (especially desirable younger viewers) bail out, the number of eyeballs (that's what we are to television advertisers) that a network is able to deliver decreases, and that further devalues each ad on television.

The third element that was missed by television executives in the first wave of the Internet was e-commerce, which allows advertisers to close the loop of marketing and sales. Because the Internet is transactional, expenditures on marketing can now be tied directly to revenues for product sales. Companies can easily correlate their advertising expenditures to sales income. This is changing television from a medium whose objective was to produce compelling content for viewers into a medium whose content serves to deliver viewers to the Web, where they may be converted from eyeballs to customers.

Simply put, media moguls now believe that commercial television's role in the future will be to deliver infomercials and other programs that will be laden with messages, web site URLs, and other embedded links to drive the viewer to the Internet for transactional opportunities. A program may be garbed as a sitcom, but it will actually be little more than an opportunity for viewers to move to the Web and learn about the stars, their clothes, and their appliances, all while watching ads and occasionally buying something. Personal interviews, non-televised extra episodes, and a plethora of other options will entice the television audience to make transactions and leave their demographic profiles, all of which translate into value for the funding advertisers.

This scenario is not necessarily the long-term outcome of television, however. Since a standard year of industrial change is likened to a month on the Internet, it is probable that the next decade will bring many fundamental modifications to both TV and the Net. Of these, the easiest to predict with certainty is that the two separate industries will finally converge, as has been anticipated since the early 1990s.

A Scenario for Digital Television

Here's a scenario for how a merged digital television/Internet might be used in a habicon during the second decade of the twenty-first century. By then, everyone in North America will have digital HDTVs because the analogue television system will have been phased out. But contrary to the prognostications of today's television manufacturers, tomorrow's sets will not be at all like the TVs we use today.

Current televisions combine electronics, a monitor screen, and a cabinet. Their price has been stable for a long time because the screen and cabinet costs have not changed significantly. The electronics comprise mainly standard components that also haven't changed much in decades. Because today's televisions are analogue, they have not succumbed to the decreasing price spiral of digital electronics.

Television sets are consumer devices, like refrigerators, and thus are built to last a long time and be relatively service-free. All of the electronics are combined on a few circuit boards, with as few connecting cables as possible (these reduce reliability as they alternately expand and contract when the set gets turned on and off). But the price you pay for high reliability and inexpensive manufacturing is a closed box that cannot be upgraded or expanded. This has not been a problem with analogue televisions because they change little from year to year. That's why a good-quality television set that is ten years old still displays a picture that rivals that of any good-quality set you can buy today.

Contrast this with the digital electronics world, where appliances normally follow Moore's law, which holds that every year and a half, the same capability becomes available for half its former price (or that every year and a half, you can buy twice the capability for the same price as before). You wouldn't dream of comparing a ten-year-old computer with a current model, for example, because it would be so inferior as to nullify the comparison.

As analogue televisions are replaced by digital ones, they will become two-part appliances. The monitor will account for the highest portion of the price, particularly for large screen sizes, and will last a long time. The electronics will no longer be built in because, as is the case with computers, they will become outmoded every few years. Digital televisions will simply be monitors optimized for program viewing and attached to specialized computers, which will replace today's set-top cable/satellite boxes and the internal circuitry of today's sets.

There are more than one hundred digital television stations now broadcasting in the United States, and by 2010 the existing TV system will be shut down. So although the near-term evolution of television will feature analogue programs overlaid with digital interactive capabilities, this model will likely become obsolete before the required new set-top boxes achieve mass-market penetration. The battle between the computer and the television set to become the preferred appliance for delivering information-age content will be over as soon as analogue televisions are phased out.

Call them what you will, the new digital TVs will be computers. This is the inevitable result of the digital revolution, whose most important legacy will be interoperability among all digital appliances. Bits are bits and bytes and bytes, and your cellphone can communicate with your laptop because they both speak the same language — on and off signals.

There will be digital connectivity to every nook and cranny of the land. Already, scientists have produced a computer, complete with an Internet browser and a URL, that fits in a microchip the size of your thumbnail and costs about ten dollars. These devices will be embedded in a wide range of appliances, from doorbells, stereos, and dishwashers to light switches, briefcases, and the clothing that we wear.

The appliance of greatest utility, however, will be the large-screen monitor that will be your portal to the Internet, your television, your videophone, your home theatre, and many other devices. You are likely to purchase as many high-quality large-screen monitors as your budget will allow. Most of these will hang on walls so they won't take up valuable room. Since they will consume wall space that is now used for hanging pictures and the like, they will probably display those same sorts of images when they are not being used for another function.

You will be able to walk over to your screen and say, "Television, please. I'd like to watch the news highlights for fifteen minutes and then the end of the *Star Trek 17* movie I was watching when I fell asleep last night." Or you might say, "Vidphone, please. Get me my mother. I think she's in Florida this week," and you would be connected to your mom. If she's not at her winter vacation condo when you call, you might hear the system respond, "No answer at home. Transferring to an audio-telephone connect." When you finally track her down on her cellphone, your greeting — "Hi, Mom. How are you doing?" — will likely be answered, "How did you find me here? . . . It doesn't matter. You have to ask how I'm doing because I haven't heard from you in two weeks . . ." Some things may never change.

Since your HAN server is a digital controller, you will be able to ask it to play a DVD movie or a commercial CD-ROM. Most likely, these will be available in the thousands on your community network for a small rental fee. Music will also be delivered through this home distribution system. At present, the record companies are fighting a losing rearguard battle to preserve their current business model, a relic of Industrial Revolution thinking. They're trying to migrate existing sales of mass-produced music CDs towards custom-recorded CDs that are downloaded and produced by listeners. This makes no sense to anyone except the entrenched industrial interests. Almost certainly, you will eventually get your recordings streamed to you on-line as you want them, without the need for making expensive physical copies.

The Internet, of course, will not be relegated to large screens or limited to computer-driven appliances; it will be available in many forms on many devices, including wrist-phones, e-books, and tele-visors (glasses with built-in heads-up displays that project a video image on the inside of the lens). However, you will still want to log into the Net from your wall screen for many activities, such as watching a sports game or other program that has a corresponding web site, which would be overlaid or windowed onto the main program.

So televisions will not be restricted to showing television programs but will become multi-purpose display devices that will perform all the functions mentioned above and more. The best part will be that every few years, you will be able upgrade your server and gain new features throughout your home.

With so many options at your disposal, you may well be wondering how you will make your content selections. The following is a reasonable guess, based in part on the telepresence trials conducted by William Buxton, Gale Moore, Ron Riesenbach, and Gerald Karam at the University of Toronto and University of Ottawa in the early 1990s.

If you've ever been at a security station in a large building, you will have glimpsed the sort of visual stimuli that new connectivity will bring. Arrayed around the security station are myriad video monitors, each displaying an image that may be of interest to the guard. Entrances and exits are featured, for example, so that comings and goings may be monitored. Parking lots, hallways, and stairwells are targeted as potential trouble spots, and there may be a roof camera to check on the weather, among other things.

Each camera does not necessarily have its own monitor. Sometimes a monitor screen is split into quadrants, with several views displayed simultaneously, and sometimes images are sequenced, one image at a time. The guard does not always see what's going on at all locations, but he has the ability to switch to any single camera position for constant monitoring when desired.

The point is that the guard is able to be aware of many separate peripheral activities at the same time, without bringing his full attention to any one. When he notices something of interest (compelling), he brings his full attention to that event and begins to concentrate on it in detail.

Similarly, your home video monitors may display many small images of news programs, sports events, movie previews, games, video-conference sites, the front door, a baby's bedroom, and so on. You will note these as you glance at the screen, and you can switch one of them to full-screen presentation if you want to participate more fully in the experience.

Did I Forget Something?

Your connection will not be limited to your home, thanks to a device that looks like a cellphone battery charger and has slots for up to a dozen memory cards, one for each member of the family. Whenever you come home, you deposit your memory card in one of the slots, which is akin to a computer's disk drive but has no moving parts. As soon as your card is inserted, the HAN recognizes your identity and updates the memory card with any calendar items, homework, house-work, phone calls, or family engagements that have been logged in your absence. Before you leave home again, you pick up your card and insert it into a mobile device, perhaps a combination cellphone/personal organizer.

Not only will your data card make its information available to you wherever you go, but it will also record any new information that comes to your mobile device, including spoken notes and instructions. So when you pass the grocery store and your gadget beeps to indicate that you are supposed to buy bread and milk, you will be able to explain that you're late for a meeting and cannot complete the task. When you get home, that explanation will be passed to others. Chances are, it still won't get you off the hook.

When you need to use your portable computer or e-book, the data on your memory card may be passed to these via a wireless link — you'll simply aim your cellphone/organizer at the book or com-puter and the devices will have a conversation and exchange the appropriate information.

Some of this may sound a bit like science fiction, but be assured that it is not. All of the features mentioned here are available today, though not in a single device. I have no doubt that by the time this book hits the stores, devices that combine several of these features will be commercially available. As a result, your residence will become much more of a home base from which your activities will naturally flow.

CHAPTER 20

Connected Commerce

E-COMMERCE HAS BECOME SO IMPORTANT SO QUICKLY THAT within a short period of time, the prefix is bound to be dropped and the simpler original word re-adopted. The reason for this is simply that most future commerce will involve digital networks in some manner. In fact, the information technology (IT) sector is already at the centre of the three major forms of e-commerce — namely, business to business, business to consumer, and business to government.

In a 1999 report, *The Emerging Digital Economy II*, the U.S. commerce department predicted that by 2006, half of all U.S. workers will be employed in the IT industry or in a field that relies on IT. Although the industry comprised only 8 percent of the nation's economic output from 1995 to 1998, it was responsible for more than one-third of U.S. economic growth. It has also helped lower the inflation rate, spark an investment boom, and increase salaries. Information technology workers earn, on average, about 8 percent more than other workers. But perhaps its most significant impact will be a change in the entire monetary system.

Our system of national currencies seems so fundamental to our society that changing it is difficult to imagine. But we should remind ourselves that it was not so long ago that areas of North America were not part of the global monetary system. Let me give you an example. In 1974, I produced a music album for the Newfoundland folk group Figgy Duff. John, the group's manager, had a university education and was cosmopolitan in his experience, but he was only a single generation away from living in a barter society. His mother grew up in a small town before there was money.

Newfoundland joined Canada as a province in 1949. Before that time, most of the outport villages relied on local fishing and hunting for sustenance. There were not many roads connecting these villages to each other or to the few large cities, so communications and commerce were restricted mainly to occasional visits by sea taxis and chartered boats. As a result, village residents used the barter system for their daily needs, exchanging meat, fish, and home-grown crops among families as required. A bad season in one of these areas meant that others in the village helped out with local credit, an example of the community banding together to ensure everyone's survival.

When John moved with his family to St. John's, the capital of the new province, they learned for the first time about poverty. Now they lived in a Canadian city that used Canadian currency, and the family's only access to food was the supermarket, which accepted only Canadian money and gave them no credit when they were going through tough times.

The fish they used to barter with their neighbours now sat in tins on supermarket shelves and could be exchanged only for dollars, which you could obtain only by working at a job. And since there were few jobs and John's parents had no training for them, the family had to get on the government dole. Welfare carried with it the terrible stigma of poverty and the destructive psychological burden of not pulling your weight in your community. In that sense, the introduction of money brought poverty to communities that had known hard times but had never been poor.

Connected communities give us an opportunity to break that monetary ball and chain. The Industrial Revolution destroyed not only many local communities, but also much of the built-in monetary support that traditionally comes with those communities. The pre-industrial towns, villages, and neighbourhoods were filled with shops and pubs where the locals were known and could get credit when times were tough. When this system disappeared, an important financial buffer disappeared with it.

Bernard Lietaer, of the Center for Sustainable Resources at the University of California at Berkeley, believes that connected communities may lead to a radical change in the nature of money. Lietaer was a central banker and a currency manager in Belgium, and he has twenty-five years of experience working with governments and banks. His book *The Future of Money: Beyond Greed and Scarcity* deals with alternative currencies and "local money" (currencies that keep resources recycled within communities).

Lietaer reminds us that money is simply an agreement within a community to use a particular medium for exchanging goods and services. Until digital networks came into use, most of us did not have the power to choose our money. But today, communities throughout North America have been experimenting with local currencies as a means of raising money for special causes. For example, civic-minded Torontonians have issued Toronto dollars to raise money for community projects. Residents and merchants sell the local bucks at par with the national currency, and they can be spent at any participating merchant. The community benefactor buys local goods with the local currency and the merchant exchanges the local currency for national currency at par.

The funds for the community projects come from a combination of unspent currency (there's always some in people's pockets) and the interest earned from the time someone buys the local bucks with real currency until a merchant cashes in the local stuff. The business model is the same as it is for traveller's cheques, though without the travelling or the chequing. And in this case, the profit goes to the local community, not to AmEx. These systems have spread throughout the United States, Australia, New Zealand, and the United Kingdom, where there are now around 300 active systems.

Digital networks may also lead to a radical change in the nature of money if certain Internet technologies are used to support the creation and maintenance of local currencies. The two mechanisms needed for maintaining a local exchange trading system are an accounting system (for keeping track of people's contributions and withdrawals) and a registry or directory (which enables people to find the goods and services they seek). Although several of these systems were created before the Internet, the emergence of Net technologies such as digital signatures and digital money makes it possible to extend them beyond local geographic boundaries. The result is nothing less than an alternative global currency that can transcend national borders. There are alternative on-line currencies in use today that allow you to sell goods and services to other participants in return for credits that you can spend on other goods and services within the on-line groups. One advantage to users is that such systems generally circumvent government taxes because the transactions do not involve money.

Community networks are a powerful means of amplifying the ability of a group of individuals to create a local currency. They offer the connectivity of the Internet with the added security that intranets bring. The computers connected to them make it possible to keep track of large numbers of transactions and inform community members of the results. And digital signatures, encrypted forms of identity, can protect against on-line counterfeiting or impersonation.

CHAPTER 21

Social Networks

A S WE MOVE AWAY FROM CITIES, TOWNS, AND FARMING COM-
munities towards connected habicons, it's only natural that our
social relationships will change as well. Barry Wellman, a professor of
sociology at the University of Toronto, believes our interpersonal
affiliations are already moving from groups to networks. When we
spoke at the Centre for Urban and Community Studies, he told me
that "although people often view the world in terms of groups, they
tend to function in networks. Most people operate in multiple thinly
connected communities as they deal with networks of kin, neighbours, friends, workmates, and organizations. Rather than fitting into
the same group as those around them, each person has his or her own
personal community."

At the same time, the social networks Wellman speaks of are influencing and being influenced by the deployment of digital networks
throughout our communities. These HANs and LANs begin in our
homes and offices, connect through local loops and community nets to
long-distance WANs, and then terminate in other homes and offices.
In the twenty-first century, these networks will all interoperate, using
the common language of bits and bytes to link any place with any other
place. More important, they will enable *people* to interoperate, linking
any person to any other person anywhere in the world. But as we've
seen, the strongest relationships are most often found in those communities that superimpose their physical place on their cyber place.

The infrastructure changes brought by the railways during the Industrial Revolution dramatically altered social and community relationships for the next 150 years. In much the same way, the infrastructure changes now being made as part of the digital revolution are altering the way we relate to each other. But there's one major difference: family and local community relationships were discouraged in the former and are being encouraged in the latter.

PART FOUR

Perspectives

CHAPTER 22

Through a Window

IN THE EARLY 1400s, THE FLORENTINE ARCHITECT FILIPPO Brunelleschi painted a picture of the baptistery of the Church of San Giovanni from the viewpoint of an observer standing inside the portal of the cathedral across the plaza. Brunelleschi's painting was not particularly remarkable because of its subject matter or the skill of the artist, but it *was* extraordinary for a different reason. Until Brunelleschi's groundbreaking work, painters had used their medium only to express stories or ideas, not the world around them. After all, how could one hope to accurately depict a three-dimensional scene on a two-dimensional surface?

Brunelleschi had found a way. Why not view a painting as a windowpane that could record the rays of light passing through it, fixing them in pigments on a panel? The image in the window could then become an image on the panel, a two-dimensional projection of a three-dimensional reality. His technique became known as the *construzione legittima* (legitimate construction), and it was used for drawing and painting by the great Renaissance artists who followed.

Brunelleschi had painted the picture of the baptistery with the assistance of technical aids — the laws of geometry, frames, compasses, scribes, and the like. These allowed him to calculate both his eye's point of focus and the invisible lines radiating from that focus, and to use these to create his visual perspective of the scene. Objects close to him loomed large. Objects far away seemed small. Round objects appeared as ovals, squares became trapezoids, and so on. The visual effect had been well known for millennia, but no one had figured out how to represent it accurately.

Perspective had not been used in the paintings of the Egyptians, the Greeks, or the Romans, all of whom held science and technology in much higher esteem than Brunelleschi's more recent predecessors. Nevertheless, he was able to represent the baptistery exactly as it appeared from the location where he had stood by constructing mathematically precise lines on the underpainting, according to rules that would produce accurate renderings for any subject material.

Leon Alberti, a renowned fifteenth-century artist, antiquarian, and man of letters, would later codify the precise mathematical and technical underpinnings of Brunelleschi's perspective work in his treatise *On Painting*. In that tome, he would write, "First of all, on the surface on which I am going to paint, I draw a rectangle which I regard as an open window through which the subject to be painted is to be seen."

Sixty years later, Leonardo da Vinci wrote about his use of a pane of glass as a transparent canvas. He described shutting one eye and tracing the image he viewed on the surface of the glass to create a perfect perspective of the scene he would paint. Soon after that, the German artist Albrecht Dürer invented a wooden frame that had silk threads running horizontally and vertically through it. He called it his net and used it to measure and capture the foreshortened perspectives of his subjects.

By the late twentieth century, computer scientists were gathering annually at the SigGraph conference on computer graphics to discuss mathematical algorithms that would do the same thing — trace rays of light as they bounced off subjects onto a screen. Computers allow scientists to abstract the process, using virtual light sources, virtual subjects, and virtual canvases, but the principles are the same as those used by Filippo Brunelleschi.

Although Brunelleschi may not have realized it at the time, one of the most important aspects of High Renaissance perspective painting was that it incorporated the body of the viewer into its spatial scheme, an important stepping stone towards what we now call immersive communication (about which more later).

Brunelleschi's invention fundamentally changed the way drawing and painting were done, and it also allowed artists to shift the perspective of how people related to their surroundings, but art alone was not powerful enough to change the relationships among serfs, feudal lords, and the communities in which they lived. Those changes had to wait for the arrival of industrialization, several hundred years later.

As we have seen, the Industrial Revolution gave birth to changes in transportation, communications, and family life that were strong enough to break the social and political frameworks of the day. It created new wealth among new segments of the population, as well as a thriving middle class. New perspectives were brought to bear on all the nooks and crannies of community living, and people began relating to each other differently.

It is sobering to realize that the changes taking place at the beginning of the twenty-first century will likely have an even greater impact than those brought by the Renaissance and the Industrial Revolution combined. Those changes, as immense as they were, originated in local regions and gradually spread throughout the civilized world. Today's changes, by contrast, are promulgated throughout the world instantly by the same connectivity that is defining the new reality.

The new windows from which we view our world are virtual, but they nonetheless express the reality around us, just as Brunelleschi's window brought his world into his view. The new connectivity creates portals through which we will redefine our relationships with family, friends, teachers, and co-workers.

The Revolution Is Dead! Long Live the Revolution!

What are the new windows through which we will be viewing the world around us? Well, the framework in which we live has been geared to an age in which factories of mass production defined our wealth and our communities: where we worked; where we lived; how we were educated; how we related to our spouses, children, gods, and governments. But that framework no longer functions, because the context in which it was crafted has changed. When you use the wrong framework to make decisions, you wind up making bad ones. The outcomes are not valid and can even be dangerous.

As an example, let's say an engineer needs to design a hovercraft. She looks through the literature and finds that scientists have proven that cats, when dropped, always land on their feet (paws, that is). It turns out that there is a biomechanical system in cats that ensures that they turn rightside up as they fall. Further research uncovers an experiment that shows why buttered toast, when dropped off the edge of a table, always lands with the buttered side on the floor (the butter alters the centre of gravity of the toast). So the engineer suggests that we strap buttered toast (butter side up) to the back of a cat and drop the saddled animal from table height. Presumably, the animal should hover over the ground as the butter and the cat's feet alternately vie for landing supremacy.

The problem with this example (aside from its absurdity) is that the contexts in which the information about the cat and the toast were generated differ from the context in which a hovercraft will operate. In this case, the reasoned deduction is neither relevant nor correct. That's why we don't design hovercrafts that way. But we do design communities, governments, and companies with information that was correct only in the now obsolete framework of the industrial age.

Like Filippo Brunelleschi, we need to find a new perspective to view our world, one whose frame of reference illuminates new relationships among people and their organizations. Using this perspective, we can give items their appropriate weights. Certain items will loom larger, while others will be less important than they were before.

CHAPTER 23

User Perspectives

A Range of Experiences

An essential difference between Internet communities and neighbourhood communities is that the former are virtual and the latter are real. These buzzwords come easily, but what exactly do they mean? How *real* is real and what exactly is *virtual*?

When I was a young musician, before digital media were available, I used to think that virtual reality was the parallel world I inhabited with my artist friends. Reality for us seemed quite different from reality as described by mainstream folks. Years later, however, I put on a helmet and goggles that placed me in a crude geometric space and a variety of very unreal-looking objects whirled about as I moved my head. The experience was supposed to be virtual reality.

Our sense of the world around us is always virtual, in fact, because we process our environment through our sensory organs. These filter the complex and myriad aural, visual, tactile, taste, and olfactory stimuli into much simpler neural signals that are interpreted by our brains in very non-linear ways. Reality, as such, may be measurable by scientific instruments, but it is not measurable by people, each of whom sees colours, smells odours, and hears sounds quite differently.

It is more useful, then, to discuss our experiences and our modes of communication in the digital age from the perspective of how we perceive them. This can be accomplished by organizing our communications experiences into four broad categories, each of which exemplifies a different level of neural processing. The categories are:

- direct
- immersive
- compelling
- peripheral

Direct experiences are what most people call reality. A face-to-face conversation and a walk in the woods are examples of direct experiences. They are not considered mediated because information reaches your senses without any intervening technology. When agents mediate our experiences and our communications, on the other hand, some of the richness and context is lost. The next three categories all describe mediated experiences.

Immersive mediated experiences envelop you and give you the feeling that you are inside the medium, instead of observing it from the outside. Examples of immersive media are three-dimensional IMAX movies and so-called virtual reality helmets, which deliver computer-generated simulations to your eyes and ears. These media do not engage the senses of touch, taste, or smell, yet they can sometimes fool the brain into thinking you are actually experiencing what they display.

Compelling mediated experiences are those that occupy your attention while presenting only a windowed projection of the world. They can be very engaging, but you are always a spectator, never a participant. Computer operating systems and software programs, for example, usually present persistent screens that require you to interact before the screen will change. They are generally compelling because interaction requires you to maintain your focus.

Peripheral experiences are the least engaging. They may be thought of as background rather than foreground, because they allow you to concentrate on other things at the same time. Listening to the radio is generally a peripheral experience, because you can drive a car or even read a book at the same time, usually without missing the content of either experience.

While some media are relatively easy to place within these categories, others present problems. For example, if you are sitting in the front section of a movie theatre, with a high density of sights and sounds enveloping you, the cinematic experience can be immersive. But when you sit in the back of the theatre's balcony, on the other hand, you experience the same movie as compelling. It will be more like *viewing* the action than being *in* the action.

Depending on the size of the screen, the distance of the viewer, and the program content, television can also present different types of experiences. When you are trying to figure out the ending of a mystery series or the missing letters in a *Wheel of Fortune* puzzle, you are having a compelling experience. But if you are glancing at *Good Morning America* or *Canada AM* while doing your morning exercises and dashing in and out of the bathroom, the experience is peripheral. In fact, many people read, talk to others, or even listen to the radio while watching television. In these cases, the experience is definitely peripheral, sort of like radio plus. On the other hand, if you watch a DVD movie on a home theatre set-up, the viewing experience is likely to be immersive, even though it's delivered through your television.

This approach of defining content by categorizing the experience of the user is opposite to that taken by most analysts of technological change. They tend to concentrate on which fibre-optic, copper, coaxial, or wireless technologies will bring the content signals to homes and offices, and on whether the PC or the TV will be the consumer appliance of choice for accessing connectivity.

I suggest it's more relevant to focus on the experiences and activities of users, those for whom being on-line must have relevance and value. This consumer-centric approach is not only more appropriate, but also goes to the heart of this book's theme, the sense of community that occurs when mediated on-line connections and direct experiences in a neighbourhood are combined. These are naturally encouraged in habicons.

Rather than looking at the Internet from the perspective of its technical delivery mechanisms, in other words, I suggest we view it from the perspective of how a user experiences the activity. And this will be very different according to whether he or she is accessing the

Net via a digital car radio or a Palm Pilot, on a desktop computer, or as part of an interactive television program. The user's interaction with the content will always be much more important than the delivery system that delivers it.

It is important to understand how individuals relate to different experiences, because critics of the Internet claim that its connectivity leads to an incomplete lifestyle and a less civil society. The direct, flesh-to-flesh contact that has become a mainstay of big-city life is being replaced by mediated connections with our families, friends, and communities, and thus it is important that we are able to predict the impacts of these new connections.

CHAPTER 24

Community
Perspectives

Education and Work

Education and training will be delivered by a combination of student-paced, location-independent on-line activities and direct experiences in schools and at work. This new way of assimilating information and acquiring knowledge will engender a new life order that is very different from the one we're following at the start of the twenty-first century.

In the coming decades, it will no longer be necessary for most of us to pursue continuous schooling until we are in our late twenties or early thirties. The great bulk of the population will begin their careers when they are in their late teens or early twenties. To be sure, there will be a small number of people who, driven by academic interests and the quest for knowledge, will attend universities in a continuous stream from primary and secondary school, and who may never enter the commercial job market. These will be our twenty-first-century monks, academics who will spend their days in re-engineered universities, institutions of renewed intellectual elitism that are no longer lumbering under the unreasonable load of having to provide long-term academic environments for the masses.

But for most of us, our careers will start earlier and consist of a series of jobs that will allow us to identify what we like to do and what we are best suited for. And we will continue our formal and informal education for the rest of our lives, according to our interests, capabilities, and job requirements. A young person with a strong drive to become a physician, for example, might enter the workforce as a part-time hospital orderly and also take medical classes part-time. Indeed, hospitals are already important institutions of medical teaching and learning because they have the required resources — doctors, patients, hospital beds, operating rooms, and the like.

Many industrial fields will similarly take students out of traditional schools. If a young person is interested in learning how to design microchips, say, where better to study than at Intel? Intel has more experts in microchip design than most universities that teach electrical engineering. An industrial placement also provides a young person with an opportunity to work and learn in the same settings where he or she may one day be pursuing a long-term career.

The advantages of this approach have been proven in the thousands of work-study programs, which have become one of the most successful initiatives of late-twentieth-century pedagogy. These programs are faint echoes of the medieval guild system of apprenticeship, though without the negative aspects of indenture and dead-ending. Their benefits are obvious: young people are exposed both to industrial culture and to the kinds of tasks and working relationships they may encounter in the future, while companies get a chance to look students over as possible longer-term employees.

The system works even better in fields where new economic growth is strongest, such as the entertainment, information management, and service industries. Companies in these fields are frequently small, sometimes start-ups, and thus do not fit the Industrial Revolution model of factories or large corporations. These work opportunities are not for everyone, of course, because they usually lack fringe benefits and job security. For some of us, however, they are a perfect fit.

For much of my life, I've been a professional composer, writing music scores for television programs and motion pictures. I have a personal corporation that handles my professional activities and those of my wife, who is a writer and producer of music events and television programs. Because many teenagers are enamoured with the thought of working in the entertainment business, our small company has been targeted for many years by local high schools as a good site for work-study programs.

Six months at Hoffert Communications dissuades most students from entering the business. They meet many extremely talented people who have a hard time making ends meet; they learn that our business is frequently feast or famine (periods of high earning interspersed with periods of no income); and they find out that when you are working on a project with a delivery deadline (which is almost always), you have to work for forty-eight or more hours at a stretch without sleep.

They meet clients who are unreasonable and sometimes obnoxious, yet to whom we must be courteous and helpful. And they learn that the major objective is to have a successful project, not just a terrific music score. Although this turns off many hopefuls, some take to it like ducks to water, and in the process they meet many clients who later give them work in the field.

Young people always ask me whether they should get a university degree or enter the business directly and gain their experience on the job. This has been a difficult question for me to answer for two reasons. First, I've been teaching film music courses at a university for almost twenty years, so I clearly place a high value on classroom instruction. Second, I believe the answer to the question often depends on the objectives, talents, and proclivities of the individual asking it. With the changes that are coming to post-secondary education, however, the answer is becoming much simpler: do both!

Although this scenario is very different from what many would consider the norm in educational strategies, it actually reflects changes that have already taken place. On average, a graduate entering the workforce today will have seven distinct jobs and employers over the course of her working life. The first job will probably be fairly closely related to her field of study, but within four years of entering the workforce, she will find that the training and skills that once were appropriate will have become irrelevant to the new tasks she now has to perform.

So why would anyone bother spending all that time in school? While there are some good answers to that question, there is also a growing feeling that for many people, formal education just doesn't make sense. One alternative is to apply the same approach to education that has been applied so effectively to many businesses. In production, it's called supply-chain management, or just-in-time inventory. The theory is that you acquire resources only as you need them, often at the last possible moment.

In education, this leads to just-in-time learning, a system that opts not to teach application-specific information until students actually need to use it. This allows students to take far fewer courses en route to certain diplomas and degrees, then pick up additional courses after they've determined which specific skills they need at work. For courses that have the greatest practical application nowadays — information technology, web commerce, and computers — this system has the added advantage of giving students more up-to-date training.

Why should you spend four years in a college computer lab when you know that the hardware and software you will be asked to use in the workplace will be a generation newer and significantly different from that which you learned on? Colleges and universities need to focus more on process, leaving the operational skills to be acquired in the workplace. When you're a student, it's a lot tougher to motivate yourself to learn a subject when you have no sense that you will ever use it. If you won't use it, you shouldn't have to take it. But if you know that the course will have a practical application, you will be much more motivated to work hard to acquire the knowledge and skill that it imparts.

For some of us, our first jobs — be they in construction, the forestry industry, or any other highly physical field — will require stamina that will be harder to come by when we are older. These jobs will not commit us to careers in these industries, but they will allow us to earn a living while learning about other jobs that may be more appropriate later in life. Once again, lifelong learning provides a solution that is difficult to find in the current system.

Of course, for such a system to succeed, employers have to make time available for workers to continue their education while still on the payroll. Interestingly, an increasing number of employers are doing just that. In fact, there is no alternative for keeping workers current in these times of rapid and drastic change. An employee who is forty years old needs to know things today that were not known by anyone when that person was twenty-five years old.

While habicons do not in themselves provide a complete solution for this change in life order, they are an important part of the systemic shift that is beginning to take place across the board, in all industries and all developed countries. Lifelong *learning* must be coupled with lifelong *earning*, however, and our new communities must help integrate family life, education, and work.

When we're speaking of the workplace today, we must take into account the home environment. More than 50 percent of North American corporations have employees who work part of the time at home. Most frequently, they use telecommunication equipment (modems, cable-modems, ISDN (Integrated Services Digital Network) lines, DSL lines) to access resources at their corporate workplace (telework). In addition, many small businesses in the service and information technology sectors operate from home offices; Internet access, fax machines, and other technologies allow them to present themselves in much the same way as businesses with separate office facilities. Habicons will enable us to pursue these new lifestyles with less stress. They will better match our living infrastructures to the variety of twenty-first-century life.

The new life order will also allow young people to marry and start families earlier than they do today. Instead of incurring debt in pursuit of a post-secondary education, young people will start earning money in their late teens and be in a better financial position when they want to have a family. In addition, if both parents are able to spend at least part of their time working from home, they will be able to care for their children without the need for and expense of daycare.

The main problem associated with teleworking has been the worker's sense of disconnection from his or her colleagues at the corporate workplace. This has often translated into an inability to forge and maintain strong team relationships. Habicons will alleviate these disadvantages with their ability to deliver large-image video conferencing and good-quality sound. These advancements will transform the tele-connection with one's colleagues from the peripheral experience it is today into a compelling and even immersive one tomorrow.

CHAPTER 25

Living in a Habicon

KEITH N. HAMPTON WAS A PH.D. CANDIDATE IN THE DEPARTMENT of sociology at the University of Toronto when he moved into our experimental habicon so he could experience life in a connected community as an insider. In his 1998 paper "Netville" (Hampton's code name for the community), he described what it was like living in the neighbourhood. He noted that messages posted to the community e-mail list formed only a small fraction of the total e-mail activity. Residents carried on many additional private e-mail conversations, sometimes supporting topics that appeared on the neighbourhood listserv but frequently on topics of interest only to the e-mail recipient.

Residents used e-mail and videophones to socialize with neighbours when weather conditions were not conducive to meeting in yards or on the street. Although Stonehaven was a new suburban development, residents knew their neighbours well and had developed friendly relationships that would have taken much longer to establish in a traditional community. Consequently, the locals had more direct social contact. There were friendly hellos, waves across the street, and informal get-togethers.

Hampton noted that this increased socialization took place despite the fact that "the neighbourhood and home plans, like most suburbs, did not encourage chance encounters. Garages are located in the front of every home, front doors are set back, and front yards are so distant from the front step that backyards are small in comparison to front lawns. In spite of these barriers, it is not unusual to see residents sitting at the front of their homes.

"[This is in contrast to] the suburban neighbourhood in which I was raised," Hampton continued. "It was very unusual to sit in your front yard or driveway. Yet, in Netville it has become commonplace for people to put chairs on the corner of their driveway, in some way substituting a front porch, or to crowd a couple of chairs onto the very small space between the top of their [outdoor] stairs and their front door."

Hampton concluded, "Initial results suggest Netville residents are using new technologies available in their home[s] to increase contact at the local level. Residents believe that they are making more ties with neighbours, and faster, than they would in a typical suburban development. Online forums such as the local email list appear to facilitate supportive relationships, local activity, and the provision of aid."

This experimental neighbourhood was built in 1996, so it is not unreasonable to question whether it has much to tell us about life in a habicon in this new millennium. But I believe we can apply some of the lessons already learned, so long as we bear in mind that:

- better technologies at lower costs will encourage more frequent use of connectivity technology;
- adults of tomorrow will have grown up using digital computers and connectivity from their earliest school days;
- human nature will not change.

Interfacing with Connectivity

Twentieth-century technologies for interfacing with digital media relied mainly on peripheral or compelling experiences. The twenty-first century will bring more immersive communications, lessening the intrusiveness of the mediating devices. This will remove much of the fear that the technologically challenged bring to new media use, and it will greatly reduce the learning curve for new users of all ages.

Today's technology designers are beginning to use natural human gestures as a means of controlling digital appliances. And, of course, voice control of appliances has been around for many decades, though it has not yet worked well enough to be of general use. I remember asking years ago for an in-home demonstration of a system that would allow my family to control the lights, the hi-fi, and other appliances just by speaking commands. We gathered eagerly in the living room as the salesperson hooked up his company's gear to our appliances.

After about an hour and a half of training the system to recognize our voices, he told me to take it for a "test drive." Since the system needed to know when we were addressing it, we gave it the name HAL, after the computer in the movie *2001: A Space Odyssey*. I cleared my throat and said, "HAL, dim the lights, please." As if by magic, the lights dimmed and we all applauded. Then I said, "HAL, raise the lights," and the lights came back up to full strength. This was pretty terrific.

Emboldened, I tried saying, "HAL, turn on the computer, please." After a short delay, the lights dimmed again. After an embarrassing pause, the expressions on our faces turned to disappointment, then to amusement. Everything went downhill from that point on. No matter what any of us said, the lights would dim; we were unable to get the system to perform any other of its promised tasks.

I am not alone in my disappointment with the technology of voice commands. While it has worked well in industrial situations, where the speaker's voice input can be carefully controlled with a headset microphone and a short list of acceptable input phrases, this technology has not met expectations during its introduction.

The situation was exacerbated by companies such as Microsoft and IBM, which introduced complicated software that purported to transform your natural speech into text that could be imported into word-processing programs or other computer applications. This was totally automated dictation without a stenographer. Unfortunately, the software never worked well.

Still, the next commercial versions of these technologies promise not to disappoint. A combination of greatly increased computer power and a better understanding of natural language and speech patterns will allow us to talk to our digital assistants much as we do to our friends, neighbours, and business colleagues. The responses will, in general, be more civil.

Yet despite all the effort that is going into developing voice and touch to control computers, the most important (and neglected) human input and output devices, as MIT Media Lab researchers noted in the early 1990s, are our eyes. One might think that tracking eye movements and converting them to useful control data would be much more difficult than using speech as the control, but the reverse turns out to be the case. Eye-tracking devices were originally developed by the military to allow fighter pilots to destroy enemy air and ground targets simply by looking at them. Today, they have made their way into such consumer products as cameras that automatically focus on the object you're looking at in the viewfinder. Amazingly, these work very well. Future habicons will use appliances that will recognize your face (yes, even with different haircuts) and allow you to move cursors and the like simply by shifting your gaze — all without the need for a mouse or other mechanical pointing device.

Computer games already use video-as-input (VAI) technologies. These interpret signals from PC-mounted video cameras and track the player's image. (They can, for example, follow the outline of a hand as it moves among regions mapped onto a computer screen.) This allows characters in games such as Vball (an onscreen volleyball game) and Club Tune (music played by cartoon mutts) to exactly mirror the motions of the game player. Because these games do not require traditional input devices, such as joysticks, trackballs, mice, or pens, the learning curve for children is not very steep. The same will hold true for adults and seniors, who will find it easier to use digital appliances, as these tools are absorbed into mainstream design.

Meanwhile, there are very significant changes coming in the way we read text. Instead of using printed books or computer monitors, we will do much of our future reading from an e-book. About half a dozen e-books were introduced into the marketplace in 1999, and although individual models suffered from deficiencies in screen contrast, form factors, weight, connectivity, battery life, and price/ performance, there will soon be next-generation products that will be very attractive to readers.

Your habicon will undoubtedly have a local wireless home network that will allow you to download books, magazines, advertisements, instructions, and other text-laden materials to your e-book. This e-book will look, feel, and read much like a printed book, except that:

- it will have only two (opposing) pages;
- you will be able to set the font size and typeface;
- you will be able to bookmark and index specific words and sections, so you can refer back at a later date;
- you will be able to move your reading material seamlessly between your computers and your e-book.

You will likely use only this single book for much of your reading, although publishers and printers will still produce coffee-table books and other books whose tactile feel or high-resolution colour printing will give them added value. This appliance will also most likely negate the need for personal digital assistants (PDAs) such as the Palm Pilot (or perhaps Palm Pilots will evolve into e-books), since it will easily display your phone book, daily calendar, and other PDA-type applications.

Because you will live in a habicon, you will be able to exchange e-book content with your neighbours, your children's teachers, and merchants in your neighbourhood. On-line shopping and direct shopping will blur, because the same e-book will display product information and pricing whether you're in a physical store or a virtual one.

As habicon appliance terminals become better able to produce a natural environment, we will use them with increasing frequency and confidence. The result will be electronically connected communities whose social frameworks may be more similar to pre-industrial life than to life in the twentieth century. Our new habicons will almost certainly be more social and immersive than the urban, suburban, rural, and farming communities that we grew up in.

CHAPTER 26

Connected Learning

THE INFORMATION EXPLOSION, CHARACTERIZED BY ALVIN Toffler as a future shock, has engulfed us in a surfeit of facts and a paucity of useful knowledge. Specialization has been increasing exponentially, making it impossible for people to keep up with all the developments in their fields. If you extrapolate the curve that plots accessible information resources, you will find that the amount of data is approaching infinity. It follows, then, that we will continue to fall further behind in our areas of interest.

There is so much to learn in any given field that going to school has become a lifelong pursuit. High schools, community colleges, universities, correspondence schools, professional workshops, Internet courses, industrial seminars, conferences — all are part of the formal learning that goes on throughout our lives. But with all the additional information we need to assimilate and organize, we spend more time at schools than ever before. The average age at which students finish their formal education has been increasing steadily, and the line between formal education and follow-on learning has blurred. In fact, 40 percent of North American adults continue to take courses after they have finished their initial formal education. Some do it to stay sharp and remain competitive, some are sponsored by their employers, and some are motivated by personal interest. If the trend were to continue unabated, we would eventually go to school until it was time for us to retire.

The gap between the age at which we are most innovative, energetic, and productive (late teens) and the age at which we enter the white-collar workforce (sometimes a decade or more later) has been widening. Women who wish to pursue a formal education often have to sublimate their desire for motherhood until they are less biologically suited to bear children. Men fit for entrepreneurial adventure must put it off until they finish school, but that is a time when they carry a high educational debt load and a burning desire to settle down and have a family, both of which argue against the risk of starting a business.

Both men and women are driven by the societal rewards of a strong career, but earning those rewards requires years of hands-on experience after they enter the workforce. The sacrifices needed often lead to the marginalization of personal life at the very time when people are getting married and starting families. These realities, along with the breakdown of strong communities and community values, were the driving forces behind the high rates of divorce in the late twentieth century.

In its final statement of the twentieth century, StatsCan released a study that supports this line of reasoning. The fertility rates in Canada and the United States are at the lowest levels ever recorded: 1.5 children, on average, per woman. The government was able to correlate the drop in births to the steady decrease in income among young earners. Alain Bélanger and Laurent Martel, two noted economic theorists, suggest in *Relative Income, Opportunity Cost and Fertility Changes*, a 1999 report, that financial constraints are preventing North Americans from keeping the fertility rate high enough for our population to replicate itself (2.1 children per woman). This has led us as a nation to rely on immigration for sustained internal growth, a policy that in the case of Quebec has serious implications for cultural sovereignty and aspirations for nationhood.

Studies throughout the world show that a lack of money is one major reason why couples in industrialized nations use contraception. Jack Wayne, a sociologist at the University of Toronto, was quoted in the *National Post* as saying, "The myth of the impoverished family with many kids is long gone." The new reality is that raising a couple of kids is a luxury that average Canadians cannot afford if they have only recently entered the workforce.

There is a bright light at the end of this gloomy tunnel, however, and for once it is not mounted on a locomotive headed straight for us. Connected communities will offer all residents opportunities to dramatically alter the structure of when, where, and how they receive their education. This, in turn, will allow young people to begin working at a much earlier age than they do today, with enormous positive consequences for industrial productivity and family living.

On-Line Learning versus Direct Learning

At the end of the twentieth century, the lead article in *USA Today* proclaimed, "Disparities [in education] are rooted not in the old divisions of race, gender or religion but in the capability of schools to deliver computers connected to the Internet." Although computers and the Internet may not be the appliances and network of choice for delivering education to our future communities, the article nailed the issue squarely. On-line learning will form the core of all education and training within a few decades. This mediated dissemination of knowledge and wisdom will be combined with direct learning in schools and in the workplace.

In 1981, Prof. Andrew Feenberg was part of the team that created what was arguably the first on-line educational program, for the School of Management and Strategic Studies at the Western Behavioral Sciences Institute in La Jolla, California. This program allowed students to discuss via their computers issues such as globalization, environmentalism, and urban planning. Peter Applebome, in a 1999 article for the *New York Times*, wrote, "Everyone figured out teaching methods and online protocol as they went along. Years later, Professor Feenberg is still impressed by the ability of online education to draw people together and interact." Despite having reservations about the corporatization of on-line learning, Feenberg believes that the quality of discussion is superior to anything he can generate in the actual classroom.

At the post-secondary level, universities and colleges are struggling to deal with a student body that is different from the one they were set up to serve. Only 15 percent of post-secondary students are eighteen- to twenty-two-year-olds who live on campus. Forty-five percent are older, non-residential students, most of whom work. In addition, there are millions of students who participate in correspondence, radio, television, and Internet courses that do not easily integrate with the activities of mainstream universities and colleges.

As the educational system changes to meet the requirements of twentieth-first-century learning, we will have to deal with the qualitative differences among experiences that are direct, immersive, compelling, or peripheral. The digital revolution is forcing us to move from technology-centred thinking to user-centred thinking, but so too is it shifting our focus away from the institutions of teaching to the students who wish to learn and be trained.

Our new connected communities will be important catalysts for the new system of education, and at the same time they will be most influenced by the education system they help to create. The key to this new education system is on-line learning.

VITAL Courses

In 1996, Don Berkowitz, the executive officer of CulTech Research Centre, and I negotiated a contract between Bell Canada and York University to create on-line course materials for distribution on the campus to York students and off the campus by Bell in commercial settings.

The name of the project was VITAL (Varied and Integrated Teaching and Learning). CulTech was nominated by both parties to design and produce the interactive content. Our team members created courses in the very different fields of computer science, sociology, fine arts, and government policy. In each case, we enlisted the help of a faculty member who was already teaching the course and was interested in using on-line materials. The course content could be used to augment direct classroom experiences or as stand-alones for off-campus learners, who could participate through a digital network connection.

Unlike correspondence courses, the VITAL courses had no textbooks or CD-ROMs. Unlike Internet courses, they made use of a wealth of video, animation, simulation, graphics, music, human speech, and other media-rich content in addition to text. The differentiating and enabling technology was a broadband network, a distribution system not then available to other course suppliers whose customers were restricted to 56K modem access.

We included excerpts from television programs, CD-ROMs, and textbooks, but these were all streamed over a special York University network and a trial network that Bell had constructed from the university to the Stonehaven West suburb for the Intercom Ontario trial.

The results were illuminating and provided insights into how future education and training programs might be delivered. Of course, since education costs make up such a large proportion of public and private spending, there have been dozens of other on-line R&D projects that tested the use of media-rich content. Some of these projects were similar to VITAL and others were quite different, yet many of the results we obtained fit well with what others had observed. For example, we found that on-line materials, when properly designed, allow students to:

- repeat, as often as needed, sections that cause them difficulty, without the stigma of falling behind the rest of the class;
- skip quickly through material that comes easily to them;
- test themselves frequently so they can get a sense of their strengths and weaknesses;
- work at convenient times (before and after traditional school hours);
- work at convenient places (home, a library, or a school facility).

The VITAL courses aimed to personalize the material as much as possible. Each course had an introductory video segment featuring a video of the course director, as well as additional video segments interspersed throughout the materials.

We gave all course directors control over how they wished to present themselves. Interestingly, none of them chose a classroom setting for any of the video segments. The conventional wisdom that students want to escape from the jail-like environment of their classrooms was taken to heart by our lecturers, all of whom went outside their classrooms for their video segments. Some of their videos were shot outdoors, some in art galleries, and some against simple, solid-coloured backgrounds. One lecturer shot all his segments in Algonquin Park. He set up the camera in the bow of a canoe and paddled around the lake while he spoke about creating web sites. All the while, his six-month-old baby was in the canoe, occasionally cooing behind an explanation of this or that.

The most difficult aspect of production was clearing the intellectual property rights for third-party materials that lecturers wanted to include. We licensed excerpts from BBC television programs, comic strips, newspaper articles, textbooks, and so on. Each of our courses required an average of more than one hundred separate clearances, and these were very time-consuming because most publishers had no history of licensing material for digital on-line delivery in an education context. By the end of the project a few years later, however, copyright collectives were beginning to form to make this type of licensing much easier in the future. Nonetheless, the issue of intellectual property rights — that is, who gets paid how much for the inclusion of pre-existing content — is a speed bump that must be overcome before high-quality on-line courses can proliferate.

Meanwhile, universities are struggling with issues surrounding intellectual property rights for material generated internally. Does the university or the professor own a course that is marketed on-line? Critics say on-line education may be less about teaching than it is about cost-cutting and replacing teachers with mass-produced software, which universities can profit from as they do from research patents. This problem will soon disappear, however, because two separate forces are acting strongly to resolve the key issues.

The first of these has caused a reversal of the classic supplier-purchaser relationship with respect to on-line courses. Traditionally, the institution and the student are purchasers of educational content — that is, they pay for textbooks, journals, images, and so on — but in the new symmetrical on-line universe, these same institutions and students will be *creating* content — in other words, they will be the suppliers. The purchasers in this scenario will range from publishers (who will wish to incorporate faculty- and student-generated text, movies, simulations, graphics, animations, photos, and sounds into their publications) to off-campus distributors (who will always be interested in expanding their catalogues).

The second force at work is technology itself. Many battles over intellectual property have arisen because the new distribution technologies do not provide an auditing trail similar to what is available when physical products are distributed from warehouses. This is a concern for publishers, who want to ensure that they will be paid fairly when their products are distributed on-line. But many of the same on-line technologies that have caused this problem will be enlisted as part of the solution. There are dozens of new companies sprouting up that specialize in the tracking and reporting of content use on digital nets.

Outcomes

What about the outcomes? Early predictions for the success of on-line learning ranged from one extreme to the other. Students would either feel alienated by the lack of direct contact, pundits said, or would relish the personal attention that can be given by a digital mentor. Our study, like most others, found that the latter is closer to the truth. It is an indictment of our education system that the ever-increasing sizes of university and college classes (a result of using cost efficiency as the over-riding administrative factor) has made the classroom experience much less personal than it used to be. Most students today do not mind the mediated experience of learning on-line, since they rarely have the one-to-one relationship with a lecturer they might prefer.

Students whose educational experiences combined both on-line learning and direct classroom learning performed best and reported having the most positive experiences. This augurs well for teachers who fear they will be made obsolete by actors who can perform better in front of a camera. On the other hand, teachers who today are not doing a good job of holding their students' attention will fare even worse tomorrow.

Students expect and need compelling experiences, and they respond even better to immersive situations that use simulations and animations that they can control and take part in. Most of us have had only the other kind of experiences at school, paying peripheral attention to what we felt were monotonous presentations that did not match our level of interest or capability.

The experimental media-rich VITAL courses are a step in the right direction. Like other educational institutions, York University has also been offering simpler text-based courses on the Internet. The student responses to these courses were studied in detail by Professors Herbert Wideman and Ronald D. Owston. They found that when students studied the same material in different settings (the classroom, by correspondence, and on-line), they had different satisfaction levels and test results. Among students with passing grades, those studying on-line scored significantly higher than their in-class counterparts. Students taking correspondence courses ranked third.

It's no surprise, then, that on-line courses are popping up at an incredible rate. Also, on-line institutions are moving beyond the obvious money-making courses, such as business administration and computer science, to offer a wide variety of courses over a wider range of disciplines. Here is just a sampling of some of the cyber-schools that are offering courses you might not be able to take at your local college or university:

- The American Military University in Virginia (www.amunet.edu), founded in 1993, offers on-line bachelor's degree programs in military studies, as well as history and intelligence studies.
- Berean University (www.berean.edu/vstudy) in Springfield, Missouri, trains students to become Assemblies of God ministers. Courses are now available on-line, with two-way live audio conferencing and audio summaries of every lesson.
- The International School of Information Management (www. isim.com) in Denver offers master's degrees over the Internet. Students must develop a Capstone Project, which is similar to a thesis but is completed on the job.
- The University of Illinois's UI-Online program (www.online. uillinois.edu) has 160 available courses, including a doctorate in pharmacy.

There are also many individuals at the digital learning frontier, including Dr. David Sonnenschein, a seventy-year-old music professor at Northeastern University in Boston. Students of Sonnenschein's Music: A Listening Experience course agree to study Mozart's minuets and Beethoven's symphonies on-line. Sonnenschein describes his course as a "stand-alone, self-paced, computer-mediated, interactive multimedia program" that is designed to introduce non-musicians to classical music.

Students listen to music, read texts, take tests, and communicate with Sonnenschein on-line. He believes that the use of technology in his courses supports his objective of teaching students how to listen and how to understand what they are listening to. He says, "I can lecture on musical forms, but to many of [my students] I might as well be speaking Chinese. But when they learn at their own pace, they can listen over and over again until the 'Aha!' happens, until they get it on their own."

For all the mythology of the importance of the classroom, many students show up and snooze rather than learn. For all the mythology of the importance of a one-to-one relationship with a professor or a teacher, most students experience classes as one-way lectures in which the teacher performs as "the sage on the stage." For all the appeal of face-to-face interaction with a lecturer, most students find the mentoring and collaborative work that are enabled with on-line learning more effective.

Distance Education Revisited

The idea of delivering education off-campus is certainly not new. Long before digital networks were able to connect students with all types of courses, schools throughout the world were delivering education and training to those who could not attend classes in person. Jim Ryan, a vice-president for outreach and co-operative extension at Penn State, says, "First, there was rural free-delivery mail, then radio, then television, then a combination of videotapes and audiotapes, and most recently, on-line education."

Britain's largest post-secondary institution, the Open University, is a prime example of a correspondence- and television-based university migrating on-line. Spread over thirty acres forty-five minutes from London, the university is home to one thousand faculty members who do research and prepare course materials for more than one hundred thousand students. BBC staff members produce accompanying television programs, videos, and CD-ROMs, which are divided into thick packets and then mailed to students.

There are no classrooms and no students on this campus. Yet the Open University has, since 1971, provided off-site education to more than 2 million students. In Britain, an off-campus student is likely to be someone who, because of his or her social or economic circumstances, is not well served by the regular university system. Ann Gall, one of these students, was interviewed by Sarah Lyall of the *New York Times* for a 1999 story on distance learning. "I had absolutely no qualifications at all," Gall said in the interview. "I was one of the people the Open University was aimed at, to give [us] a second chance." Gall, who is in her fifties, left school in Birmingham at fifteen, had a family, and worked in secretarial positions. In 1983, she enrolled in the Open University and began studying in her spare time towards a university degree. She would begin her schoolwork at 5 a.m. and work until her children got up for breakfast. She also studied late into the night while her children slept, and worked at her courses during weekends and on vacations.

In addition to the personal satisfaction she gained, Gall earned a promotion at work. But, having been bitten by the learning bug by then, she eventually decided to become a full-time student and pursue a Ph.D. in geology at the University of Birmingham. Today, she continues to take supplementary courses through the Open University.

In 1999, the Open University migrated to the United States. In North America, where university attendance has almost become a right of any citizen, administrators expect most Open University students to be sent by employers who want to upgrade their employees' skills while keeping them on the job.

In Britain, the Open University has been much more successful than American-style correspondence schools because its courses are carefully designed from scratch, use a variety of media, and are very well researched and produced (they cost about $2 million apiece). The university also has 300 locations throughout the United Kingdom where students can interact directly with tutors on a face-to-face basis. The combination of high production values and direct tutoring has created an excellent track record.

The challenge now is to move this personal interaction and television-based model to the Web. The hope is that the lack of direct student-to-mentor contact will be counteracted by video conferencing, chat, and e-mail, applications that will allow students greater access to tutors than they would typically have on a campus.

On-Line Encyclopedias

In the future, not all learning materials will have to be generated from scratch. Vast information and research resources already exist in the form of books, periodicals, documentaries, television programs, newspaper and TV news archives, and the like. One by one, these are being recast as resources for on-line learning and research.

The Encyclopedia Britannica has long been the single most popular resource for high-school students. By taking its publication on-line, Britannica has provided an example that other publishers of reference materials are beginning to emulate. Since 1998, the encyclopedia set has been available only on-line. Initially, the company racked up sales by offering Internet subscriptions at a fraction of the price of its printed books, but then it changed its business model to make the encyclopedia's contents available free to all Internet users. The company now earns its revenue from web site advertising, and many advertisers are eager to associate their names and products with the huge number of readers who look to the web site for information.

The Encyclopedia of Music in Canada (EMC) is an example of a more focused resource. It has gone through two print editions, each of which cost about $2 million to produce. But as is the case with most printed material, it was out of date as soon as it came off the press. And because books become unwieldy if they have too many pages, print editions are limited in size and hence in the number of topics they can cover.

The EMC had focused primarily on classical music because of the space limitations of its English and French print editions. In the book world, information is a zero-sum game. In the case of the EMC, this meant that for every page that was devoted to pop music, one more page was unavailable for classical music (or any other genre). As a result, the jazz, pop, film music, aboriginal, and other musical communities were miffed by the encyclopedia's less-than-thorough-treatment of their genres.

In 1998, this non-profit music encyclopedia decided to break with tradition and cease publication of its print editions. Instead, EMC opted to publish on-line. The thousands of existing articles were supplemented with music clips; music scores; photographs of musicians, composers, and concerts; concert posters; and videos. Many additional thousands of articles on previously underrepresented musical genres will make the encyclopedia more comprehensive and valuable to users.

These on-line encyclopedias can be updated daily, instead of once every decade or so, and thus are becoming repositories of current happenings as well as historic events. Most important, they will no longer be limited to libraries, academic researchers, and those families who can afford the high purchase price. For the first time in history, research resources that are expensive to produce can be made available to everyone, an added-value resource for learning in a habicon.

CHAPTER 27

Arts and Entertainment

O UR HABICONS WILL BE FULL OF CULTURAL EXPERIENCES, much more so than the home of the twentieth century, which relied most heavily on television for cultural connections and entertainment. When they are not out having direct experiences, children will likely receive their stimulation from the successors to today's video-game units. Nintendo, Sony, Sega, and Microsoft (with its upcoming X-Box) will vie with Dell, Apple, Compaq, and IBM to be the suppliers of choice for the young generation. This market already boasts greater annual sales than the entire Hollywood movie industry.

The new video-game consoles will connect to your wireless home network and will be able to access many of the same applications and content as the wall-mounted and television monitors you will have positioned throughout the house. Your digital televisions and video-game units will both be powerful computers, one designed to harmonize with a family viewing environment, the other with a child's play environment.

On blustery cold days, a young child may want to stay at home and play an interactive video game with Sally down the block or George across town. His parents may want to do the same later that evening, except that their game will be bridge, configured so that the other players will be visible on a large wall screen while a close-up of their playing cards shows up in their personal e-books.

The most popular form of entertainment will continue to be

music, followed by television programs and movies. Most of these will be delivered on demand, however, which will allow users to program the equivalents of their own radio and television channels. The biggest coming change in entertainment is that it will soon be able to emanate *from* a habicon home, not just be delivered *to* it.

Distributed Music Performances

In 1969 (as mentioned earlier) I co-founded Lighthouse, a rock band that had considerable success recording and touring around the world. Lighthouse disbanded in 1975, but the group re-formed in 1995 to record a new album and perform once again for audiences.

For the most part, we perform with all ten of our band members in a single location. But in 1996, I had the opportunity to combine my research interest in connected communities with a concert that tested networked collaboration among artists. Lighthouse had been hired to play at the closing ceremonies of the Smart Cities International Conference, and the organizers asked if we would consider using advanced network technology to try a distributed performance.

I jumped at the chance, and was encouraged by the reaction of my bandmates, who were game to try a new and challenging way of performing. After consulting with our technology partners, Rogers Cablevision and Bell Canada (in one of their infrequent collaborations), we came up with a concept that placed half the band at the closing ceremonies of the conference facility and the other half some thirty kilometres away.

At each location, the remote band members were telepresenced to the performing band. On each stage, sound monitor speakers allowed us to hear our remote colleagues while a large screen behind us allowed us to see them, life-size. The sound mixer at each location received separate feeds from each remote player and mixed them with the live sounds — business as usual for these fellows.

Each of the two simultaneous concerts was half virtual and half real — or to use the language at the start of this section, it was both a direct and a compelling experience — because the remote players vied for the audience's attention with the live musicians. The quality of the audio and video was less than stellar, but the audiences at both locations loved it, and we all had a feeling that we were beginning to tap into a mode of collaborative performance that could have many important implications.

The Japanese delegates to that conference were members of the 1998 Olympic planning committee, and they used our "distributed performance" idea for the Olympic Games' opening ceremonies, during which Seiji Ozawa conducted choirs and orchestras around the world in Beethoven's Ninth Symphony.

For that performance, Ozawa and the members of his orchestra in Osaka were a self-contained unit — they could not hear any of the remote ensembles. The other musicians around the world played along with feeds of the Ozawa performance, which arrived via satellite with different delays (some more than two seconds) at each location.

To mix this into a coherent television program, technicians had to delay the original Osaka signal so that the later-arriving signals could catch up to it. Each remote location had its own compensating delay. In effect, the viewing audience witnessed an electronically synchronized round-the-world link-up, even though the individual components were occurring at slightly different times.

After the Smart Cities conference, I organized a more ambitious series of collaborative performances for the Interactive '96 conference in Toronto. These performances included visual artists, dancers, and an inter-city–distributed jazz band. Buffy Sainte-Marie, the First Nations pop star, *Sesame Street* regular, and visual artist extraordinaire, was one-half of a visual arts tag team. The other half was the painter Rae Johnston, who created a canvas in real time during the conference gala. Its image was sent forty kilometres to a distant computer work-station, where Sainte-Marie modified it using Photoshop, a digital image-editing program. This altered image was then sent back to Johnston, who referenced it as she continued her work. The result was a collaborative canvas, the product of two artists interacting over dis-tance to produce a single work that, in this case, was quite beautiful.

At that same conference, Keith Holding and Michael McHale, pioneers in the integration of television and new media, came up with the concept of producing a pas de deux by digitally integrating two solo dancers, each in a different location. One was black, and was clad

in black against a white background, and the other was a pale Cau-
casian, clad in white against a black background. Richard Cortes
designed the dance concept and Holly Small choreographed it so that
a computer could process the two images and combine them into a
single large image for the audience at each location. In that combined
image, each dancer's body could be made to disappear by moving it
into the background zone of the electronic image.

The dancers rehearsed using the digital imaging technology so
that they could see the effects of their movements on monitors that
displayed the integrated images. The work evoked strong and positive emotional reactions from the live audience on the evening of
the performance.

Still, the experiment did have some glitches. The electronic processing that compressed the video images so they could fit into the
available communication "pipes" resulted in a time delay of about
one-quarter of a second. While this was not a significant factor for the
visual artists or the dancers, the members of the jazz group I had
assembled had a rough time adjusting.

I had stationed a bass player and a drummer in Montreal, a

saxophone player and a trumpet player at the Bamboo Club in Toronto, and a guitar player at York University. I was at a grand piano in the Citytv/Bravo! television studios. Visuals from the four locations were combined electronically so that we could each see and hear the other members of the band. To play in sync, we each had to perform one-quarter of a second *ahead* of the music we heard from our speaker monitors. That was the only way our sounds could be combined so the audiences would hear a single integrated performance. This was extremely difficult to do in a consistent manner. In fact, we were unable to do so at the dress rehearsal, but when the adrenaline began to flow during the actual performance, we pulled it off.

But what is the point of these experiments? Well, no one is suggesting that future performances of symphony orchestras will take place in one hundred cities simultaneously, with one musician live in each location (although that will be possible). But there are countless practical applications that come to mind. For example, a young cellist living in a small community may one day be able to practise string quartets with other musicians of her calibre who live in distant cities. Advanced music students scattered throughout the world will be able to take master classes with renowned soloists using telepresence instead of having to travel to where these virtuosos live. The ramifications for community living are enormous. You will no longer have to live in London or New York to participate in arts activities that today require residence in or travel to those locations.

CHAPTER 28

Family Perspectives

Where Is Everyone?

Modern families often have trouble keeping track of members' whereabouts. Today, moms, dads, and kids all have their own schedules chock full of things to do. Work, school, music lessons, sports, exercise clubs, doctor appointments, pet-grooming appointments, friendly get-togethers, and family events occupy us on a day-to-day basis. It's tough to keep track of who's doing what and when, particularly because our schedules change daily.

Vacation periods are different from one school to another, and from one workplace to another. Appointments with professionals are at the convenience of the practitioner, not family members. To make things more complicated, there are long weekends, holidays (observed by some companies but not others), and unpredictable extra work hours and workdays. So how can you plan a family outing when you don't know where all your family members will be, or how long they will be where you think they are?

The problem boils down to poor communication of schedules within the family group. It is a relatively new problem, born of times when most family members are more occupied with solo activities than they have been in the past and exacerbated by the lack of a single homemaker who's dedicated to keeping track of family activities.

Fortunately, the problem can be solved by software and connectivity, as it has been in the workplace. At work, the same sorts of scheduling problems occur, but they are handled by computers that run shared calendar programs and are connected by the office network. At companies that use these tools, each employee maintains a local activity calendar and can mark entries as public or private. The public entries can be viewed by all who need to see them, so that setting up an appointment or group conference is relatively easy.

Yet even though more than half the homes in North America now have computers, these are not generally used for coordinating family members' activities. There are several reasons for this, the chief one being that home computers are not usually located in high-traffic areas, where they'd be easily accessible to all members of a family. The den, bedroom, and home office are the most common locations for computers today, but these are not places where all family members hang out. On the other hand, the kitchen is at the crossroads of family traffic flow but doesn't normally house a computer. Even when it does, that computer may not be linked to other computers in the house.

Another stumbling block is that many of us are still technologically challenged or rooted in pre-digital thinking. The idea of scheduling family activities through an electronic device instead of just yelling from room to room seems ludicrous to some. But the ability to see at a glance when birthday parties and other family obligations are scheduled is a godsend for those who use these systems because it allows them to easily organize and prioritize their ever-dwindling discretionary time.

Every six months, companies release a raft of new consumer appliances and devices that make better use of digital technology and connectivity. It will not be long before families are using these new and generally wireless communications devices throughout their homes, carrying some of them as they walk out the door. Our homes, as we've seen, already have wired networks for telephones and televisions. By the end of the first decade of the twenty-first century, these wired networks, along with their wireless counterparts, will interoperate seamlessly, enabling "plug and play" versatility whenever a new device is released into the marketplace.

Throughout the 1990s, telephone, cable-TV, Internet, and satellite companies were all crowing about how they would be the suppliers of residential digital content, yet none had dealt with the fundamental problem of how to distribute that content within an apartment or a home. In an effort to remove that roadblock, the electronics industry has come up with several new wireless home-networking products that can send content from any entry point throughout a house or an apartment, all without the need to break down walls, install wires, repair the damage, and then repaint.

These breakthrough home networks are paving the way for a slew of new interconnected appliances that will be much more affordable and convenient than computers. The simplest of these are personal information managers (PIMs), a combination of our modern-day phone books, appointment schedulers, and notepads. The next generation of PIMs will spill their information (provided the user authorizes it) into the home network so that others can share schedules and such.

This transformation of home area networks will allow for the integration of many appliances that are separate today and will lead to a truly smart home. The "smart home" concept has been bandied about for decades, but as was the case with Dick Tracy's wrist radio the idea had to wait until we had the technology to make it a reality. That technology is available today.

The key ingredient needed to bring a home fully into the digital era is connectivity — that is, the ability to connect all home systems and appliances to each other and to global networks. Such global connectivity will allow you to control your home from any location, and will also enable authorized monitoring from a remote location (from your security service, say).

If you run low on heating fuel in your smart home, a truck will automatically show up with a refill, having been alerted to your need by a sensor in your fuel tank. Internet refrigerators will automatically order more eggs or soft drinks from your local Internet grocer when the relevant compartment nears empty. The same could hold true for foodstuffs in your pantry and toilet paper in your bathroom closet, provided their labels are fitted with electronic identifiers that can be read by an inventory device in your closet.

Not everyone will want to go to the trouble of programming an automated home inventory system, of course, but there will be other features that will appeal if that does not. For example, almost every new homebuyer is interested in having a home security system. But those systems, although digitally controlled, have not generally been able to interoperate with other home systems. The lack of integration among security systems, entertainment systems, e-mail, telephones, television sets, and general Internet access is not a technical issue. These systems are all digitally controlled, and digital telephones and televisions are beginning to worm their way into many homes as well. In other words, it's not technology that has been the impediment to really smart homes but the lack of coordination and co-operation between industrial sectors, which fear losing some of their exclusive consumer base to new competitors.

With the convergence of industries, appliances, and media, however, it will no longer matter what an individual industry wishes to do, since any other industry — or even an independent start-up company — may be able to gain control of digital appliances and integrate their operation. The result is that these stand-alone product and service companies are being dragged — kicking and screaming, in some cases — into the digital age.

Here's an example of a neat smart home feature that could have been introduced half a decade ago to homes with Internet access if industries had agreed to co-operate. It will likely be available in most habicons.

Let's say someone comes to the door of your apartment or house. A video camera mounted above the door makes his or her image available to be displayed on any television, computer, or other monitor screen in your home. If you're at home, you can have a conversation with the person before you open the door. If there's no one in, that fact will register with your smart home controller (the same sensors that turn the lights on or off when people are present in a room will report that no one is home).

If the house is empty, the door camera will snap a picture of your visitor and send it over an Internet e-mail link to your local appliance, which may be a computer in your office or a cellphone/organizer/

e-mail gadget in your purse or briefcase. You'll get an alert that might read something like this: "Excuse me, there's somebody at the front door of your house. Shall I send a prepared message, or would you like a direct speech link?" Depending on who you see and what you are doing at the time, you may well decide to send an instruction that will trigger a prepared response. "I'm not home now," an automated attendant may say to the person at your front door. "At the beep, please leave a brief video message and I'll get back to you as soon as possible." That video can then be accessed either remotely or when you're back at home so you can follow up. It will also be stored, along with videos from other strategically placed cameras, for review in the case of a break-in. More expensive set-ups will stream the video constantly to security services that will monitor your property.

The Elderly and the Challenged

Those who will likely gain the most from habicons are also those whom the Industrial Revolution has marginalized the most: the elderly. Seniors generally have much more time to spend configuring their living environments and leisure time. That's why they are such a growing and important segment of Internet users. As the elderly become more comfortable with digital appliances such as computers, they will begin to create an enormous range of applications for themselves and their peers. These applications will make tomorrow's habicons much safer and more comfortable for seniors.

For example, a habicon home with seniors in residence will chirp alarms at the times when medication needs to be taken. The system will keep track of how much has been consumed and when new supplies must be ordered from the drugstore. In addition, simple reminders about birthdays and anniversaries of friends and family members will allow those whose memories are failing to keep in touch at happy times, emphasizing their thoughtfulness instead of their memory challenges.

The most common complaint from the elderly is that they are lonely. This is particularly true for those who live alone. For them, mediated communications will be a godsend, especially when the alternative is no communication at all. Audio and video messages to friends, family, social workers, and physicians who may be on one's mind at 2 a.m. will be sent while thinking is coherent, even though the recipients will not pick up the missives until waking or office hours.

One of the best features for seniors will be mediated socializing. Seniors will be able to play mah-jong, bridge, or checkers with friends who may live only a few blocks away, but for whom the visit in inclement weather may be too arduous. For family members, the value of checking in on a parent via video telephone and being able to see the expression on the parent's face will greatly outweigh the modest cost of such a service.

Those who have physical or mental disabilities will also be major beneficiaries of connected communities. Assistance and services that would normally require travel, either by the person in need or by a health or social worker, can be made available in the home, greatly increasing the frequency of such assistance and greatly reducing the cost.

Rooms with a View

I had the opportunity to experiment with connected social experiences when I was the executive director of the Intercom Ontario trial. Once the Stonehaven neighbourhood network became operational, we decided it would be a shame to restrict the interactions of habicon residents to only their own small group. Wouldn't it be exciting, I thought, to connect them to activities outside their suburb, to the downtown action that they normally miss out on? In 1997, my colleagues and I were able to configure just such an experience.

Each September, Toronto hosts the largest international film festival in the world. Thousands of film and television personalities descend on the city to promote and watch hundreds of films from around the globe. With the assistance of Citytv, a consortium member, we came up with an idea that would allow suburban residents to be part of the action.

The InterActive '97 Conference, which was also being held in Toronto that year, staged a virtual party, aptly named a cyber-soirée, to connect several real communities with each other and with Internet communities around the world. The concept was simple enough:

throw a few parties at locations across the continent with the common theme of celebrating movies; connect the party-goers with high-speed fibre-optic and satellite connections so they can interact with live images of other celebrants at all locations; and coordinate all events with the Toronto Film Festival.

Each partying group could interact with any other group using video cameras and large video screens. All locations shared a merged audio-visual experience (a four-way split screen), and each shared its own local activities. Suburbanites rubbed shoulders with high-profile politicians and entertainment celebrities, and live entertainment at each location was available to every other location.

The integrated experience was webcast by CityInteractive so that interested netizens could share in an abridged version of the events. CityInteractive spiced up its live webcast with additional festival-related quizzes and interactive games for both soirée participants and folks who simply "tuned in" on the Net.

In the Stonehaven West neighbourhood, family and neighbours gathered in Bob Penman's home. For the first time in their lives, they were able to hobnob with the glitterati, as well as be part of the glitz and glamour of the film festival and the exclusive festivities at the other party sites.

In downtown Toronto, meanwhile, revellers gathered at an eatery called Joe's Elbow Room. Attendees included representatives from the film, news media, and television industries. This noisy but cheery bar-room had been outfitted with television monitors, computers that were logged into the live Internet feed, and professional-quality video and audio equipment for sending and receiving images to the other sites.

The Academy of Canadian Cinema and Television hosted the Los Angeles party at the official residence of Kim Campbell (the Canadian consul general and former prime minister). Joe Meldrum, an Apple Computer executive who attended the party in L.A., reported that "the attendee list included high-profile entertainment industry executives, actors, and comedians. . . . We demonstrated video conferencing, interactive CD, and CD movies."

At the Citytv schmoozefest party, the broadcast visionary Moses Znaimer provided a live feed of the activities of the more than one thousand celebrants. This party was also broadcast live over conventional television, with occasional feeds from the CityInteractive folks.

It is difficult to express in words the effect of bringing all these people together. From the moment we went live with split screens of the Honourable Kim Campbell's swimming pool in Los Angeles and the Penmans' kitchen in Stonehaven, we all shared a single vision:

- *we* can be on TV;
- *we* can transcend space;
- *we* can influence distant events.

The following is an excerpt from the live webcast:

First participant: We are all in one neighbourhood. We are all connected, and we all talk to each other on a regular basis.
Second participant: With this society now, everybody is working at such a fast pace. You come home from work, you don't have time to socialize. This way, it only takes minutes to socialize. You can get on-line

with your videophone, and you can talk to your neighbours and get updated as to what everybody is doing in the neighbourhood.

Over the course of the evening, demonstrations of habicon connectivity gave party-goers a glimpse into the future. A hearing-impaired child who lives in the habicon, for example, "spoke" via videophone with his special-needs teacher using sign language. For him, it was the first time he was able to "talk" on a phone.

The technology needed to pull off this cyber-soirée in 1997 was immense. We had to set up a television control centre at the Bell Canada central office, where the fibre-optic lines and satellite feeds were routed. The analogue television signals were digitized, but even then they did not easily interoperate with the digital Internet signals, which used different protocols. In Los Angeles, the consul general's residence was not near a fibre-optic line, so we had to rent a remote television news truck and send the signals up to an orbiting communications satellite for eventual integration with the land signals.

Morgan Earl, our Emmy Award–nominated producer, later said, "The cyber-soirée was one of the most technically complex live television productions I've ever worked on, but the result was absolutely worth it. Although we sweated, screamed in our headsets, and crossed our fingers throughout the evening, the party-goers seemed really relaxed and just enjoyed themselves. For them, the physical separation of the locations vanished as easily as it does on a phone call. The expressions on the faces of our participants make me think that, once the technology becomes routine and inexpensive, people will insist on having this capability."

It will be available sooner rather than later. In early 2000, I began designing a new Digital Media Institute with Dr. Ron Baecker, a colleague at the University of Toronto. We wanted to connect many different universities, colleges, and public access sites with the same sorts of multi-point video link-ups we had had at the cyber-soirée. Amazingly, technology had advanced so much in the three intervening years that our technical consultant told us we could accomplish everything we'd done at the film festival with off-the-shelf equipment at a fraction of the cost.

By the end of the second decade of the twenty-first century, people will wonder what all the fuss was about. The huge industry-driven debates about how to design program content for interactive television will be forgotten as communities and individuals experience the ease of coming together outside the controls of the television and telephone industries, using private and community-controlled resources to set up their own instantly configurable connected events.

Social Communities

For most of us, sex is like that old soft drink slogan: "There's nothing like the real thing!" However, the threat of sexually transmitted diseases and the anonymity of the Internet have made that medium a favoured place for sexual encounters that feature images and sounds but no physical contact or personal risk. Although sex-related sites are the most popular on the Internet, they do not offer much opportunity for people to form lasting relationships. And yet direct relationships are still what we crave most.

Habicons are much more satisfactory than the Internet in this area. They offer new opportunities for us to meet our social partners. Although co-workers, church members, and friendly matchmakers will continue to be important agents for bringing people together, a connected community will combine the resources of newspaper personals, an Internet dating service, and a TV program like *Love Connection*. As more and more couples meet within the mediated safety of a video-capable network, blind dates may well become a thing of the past.

Religious Communities

Even religious institutions will need to change as a result of habicon life. To understand what their new role will be, we should look to the trend towards separating religious experiences from the practice of religion. The relationship we have with God is no longer necessarily inseparable from the relationship we have with our church, as Karen Anderson detailed in her 1993 best-seller, *A History of God*.

Many experience their relationship with God as a spiritual connection with a supernatural power. On the other hand, churches are manifestations of God's government on earth, and as such are run by human beings and subject to the frailties of all secular organizations. While there has been a significant increase over the past thirty years in the number of people who believe in God — more than 90 percent of North Americans now claim to hold that belief — attendance at churches has declined steadily over that same period. This is the result of the erosion of the intermediary role the church usually plays between the supplier (God) and the consumer (the worshipper). In fact, a majority of American Christians describe themselves as born-again, a form of Christianity that requires a direct relationship with God and a reduced reliance on traditional church intermediaries. This trend is consistent with the general disintermediation that took place in late-twentieth-century life.

TV and radio evangelists began to erode the central role of physical churches even before the Internet came on-line. For the past several decades, in fact, these media preachers have given viewers and listeners a great range of personal religious expression; you can change the channel until you locate a religious message that suits you. On the Internet, users have had even greater choice over religious material. They can read the sacred texts of their choice on-line, research passages, and purchase religious paraphernalia directly.

The challenge for churches is essentially the same challenge facing businesses and governments. They must find a way to re-intermediate themselves by adding value for consumers (worshippers) within the new context of connected communities. Some of the attempts to do this, however, have not met with the acceptance of traditional churches. For example, PiousNet's home page features a salvation-on-demand service billed as Compufess, "the on-line confessional for the sinner on the go." The televangelist Randall Sinclair Prescott describes its advantages succinctly: "Whether you inhaled a controlled substance, embezzled money from your employer, or poisoned your neighbour's barking dog, now you need not burn in hell."

Sinners can atone from the privacy of their homes, for the low price of just $2.99 per confession. All they have to do is type their sins into the computer. The software program on the web site, purported to be inspired by God, then analyzes the bad thoughts or deeds and computes the appropriate penance in seconds, be it one hundred Hail Marys, fifty Acts of Contrition, or seventy-five Glory Be's.

Margaret Wertheim, in her book *The Pearly Gates of Cyberspace*, compares the Internet itself with a church. She writes, "Where early Christians conceived of Heaven as a realm in which their 'souls' would be freed from the frailties and failings of the flesh, so today's champions of cyberspace hail their realm as a place where we will be freed from the limitations and embarrassments of physical embodiment.

"No words can explain the 'place' that is nowhere, the 'point' that is everywhere. No metaphor can describe the fusion of body and soul into Oneness that for medieval Christians was the source of everything. At the moment of this beatific vision, language at last fails one of its greatest exponents. Body-space and soul-space have been melded into one space. The mystery is beyond intellection."

Conclusion

Having ended this book with a look at how religions are coping on-line, it seems worthwhile to revisit the Amish criterion for evaluating technology, which we examined at the beginning of this book. The Amish deem a technology "good" if it brings their community closer together. By this measure, our twenty-first-century communities, when they are connected by locally controlled networks — our habicons — will indeed be beneficial.

Habicons may make it possible to reverse many of the desocializing effects of the Industrial Revolution. They encourage increased family cohesion and communication and help re-establish the trusting relationships that come from knowing your neighbours and your neighbourhood.

As technology advances, our Internet portals will become much more adapted to natural human languages, and thus much more immersive. Large screens will display realistic life-size images and will interoperate with communications and computing devices that will be embedded into our clothes, cars, homes, and offices. These will make our on-line experiences more natural and compelling, and will ultimately culminate in our ability to move among our worlds of interest as easily as the fictitious character Martin Silenus does among his real worlds of interest in the science-fiction novel *Hyperion*.

In that book, the author, Dan Simmons, has Silenus describe the connected communities that stem from the portals in his home:

> *My home has thirty-eight rooms on thirty-six worlds. No doors: the arched entrances are farcaster portals, a few opaqued with privacy curtains, most open to observation and entry. Each room has windows everywhere and at least two walls with portals. From the grand dining hall on Renaissance Vector, I can see the bronze skies and the verdigris towers of Keep Enable in the valley below my volcanic peak, and by turning my head I can look through the farcaster portal and across the expanse of white carpet in the formal living area to see the Edgar Allan Sea crash against the spires of Point Prospero on Nevermore. My library looks out on the glaciers and green skies of Nordholm, while a walk of ten paces allows me to descend a short stairway to my tower study, a comfortable, open room encircled by polarized glass which offers a three-hundred-sixty-degree view of the highest peaks of the Kushpat Karakoram, a mountain range two thousand kilometers from the nearest settlement in the easternmost reaches of the Jamnu Republic on Deneb Drei.*
>
> *The huge sleeping room Helenda and I share rocks gently in*

the boughs of a three-hundred-meter Worldtree on the Templar world of God's Grove and connects to a solarium which sits alone on the arid saltflats of Hebron. Not all our views are of wilderness: the media room opens to a skimmer pad on the hundred and thirty-eighth floor of a Tau Ceti Center arctower and our patio lies on a terrace overlooking the market in the Old Section of bustling New Jerusalem. The architect, a student of the legendary Millon DeHaVre, has incorporated several small jokes into the house's design: the steps go down to the tower room, of course, but equally droll is the exit from the eyrie which leads to the exercise room on the lowest level of Lusus's deepest Hive, or perhaps the guest bathroom which consists of toilet, bidet, sink and shower stall on an open, wall-less raft afloat on the violet seaworld of Mare Infinitus.

At first the shifts in gravity from room to room were disturbing, but I soon adapted, subconsciously bracing myself for the drag of Lusus and Hebron and Sol Draconi Septem, unconsciously anticipating the less than 1-standard-g freedom of the majority of the rooms.

Because he lives in a science-fiction book, Silenus can do something we cannot, and that is walk through his portals into the worlds he sees. Although we may never have that capacity, we are rapidly approaching a world in which similar mediated experiences will be part of our day-to-day lives.

Index